HIDING IN PLAIN SIGHT

Burt Harding

in the garden Publishing

a media company of

WHAT WOULD LOVE DO INT'L LTD

ISBN: 978-0-9855314-0-9
Library of Congress data available upon request.

Cover and Interior Design by Christine Horner

Published by:

IN THE GARDEN PUBLISHING
P.O. Box 752252
Dayton, OH 45475

www.InTheGardenPublishing.com
www.WhatWouldLoveDoIntl.com

Printed in the United States of America

Appreciation for

HIDING IN PLAIN SIGHT

Dear Burt,

Thank you for the book. I have just read 20 pages and already I feel the book's impact. I feel free from some of the concepts I've had and more importantly, I can feel it in my heart that your book is true."

~~ ***Jane*** *(Florida)*

Hi, Burt,

For a long time my body has been so contracted I could barely read a few pages out of a book before my eyes would start to hurt, but I am really starting to get how you meant nothing is personal. As I got only on page 14 in your book and really read with an open heart, something really started to hit me. I started to see clearly how you can't escape this moment and to just receive what is given, knew it in my heart; everything was allowed without any effort on my part and really felt all the past pain starting to diminish. Thank you so much for sending this book."

~~ ***James Ngo***

Hi, Burt,

Thank you for your...booklet. I am an avid reader of metaphysics and Advaita teachings. Reading your book touched me in a way that went deep inside me. It lingered even after closing off the computer. I find myself more aware than ever before with a greater feeling of confidence. I can't thank you enough.

~~ ***Norm Sleep***

Well, I finally finished reading Hiding in Plain Sight *last night and WOW – it was fantastic and you are just so good at explaining things. I feel I understand more and ever new things are dawning in me about 'Being' and how living in pure Awareness is the only real way to live!*

~~ ***Karen Butler***

CONTENTS

FORWARD

in the garden Publishing believes *Hiding in Plain Sight* is one of the most powerful books on the planet in contemporary form for awakening human consciousness.

As such, we made the decision to honor the text as it was received through Burt Harding as a Gift from Holy Spirit, editing it sparingly.

At the appearance of additional line breaks, you are invited to pause to allow for the fullness of the experience and reflection.

INTRODUCTION

This book was written through an inspired moment one morning. The strong urge to sit down and write it was not something I could control. I feel confident that if it is read with an open heart it will bring a shift in consciousness.

If you make it all the way to the end of the book with unwavering interest then clarity is assured.

With love,
Burt

PART I

CHAPTER ONE

Our Intuitive Heart

Picture a Mexican man crossing the border to the United States on his bike, carrying a heavy bag on his back. The border patrol stops him as a lot of smuggling goes on between Mexico and America. When asked what he is carrying he says, "Sand!" Upon inspection it is true. They let him through. This happens again and again.

One day the policeman quits his job at the border. Having a drink at the local bar, the Mexican walks in. The policeman says, "I have seen you at the border and since I am not a policeman anymore, I won't report you, but I have a strange feeling you're smuggling something. We're friends now, just tell me."

The Mexican replies, "Bicycles."

In a way, the secret is hidden, yet it is totally obvious. The truth is obvious, but not to the conditioned mind. Our intuitive heart when awakened, will marvel at how obvious it is in this, **THIS** very moment.

All and everything is Oneness, and all we do is get in its way by trying to find it. How can you find that which you already are?

All you need do is **SEE**. The hope is that this book will help you to see what is obvious.

When awakening happens, people say more than anything else, is that what is now seen is totally obvious.

We are now living at a time when awakening is rampant among most sensitive intuitive humans.

You *think that* you are seeing me. In fact, all that is really happening is that there is the seeing of me; of whatever it is that's arising. The difference between awakening and not awakening – between seeing and not seeing – is simply the seeing that there is no one there. There is no "me".

CHAPTER TWO

MY WORK AS A PHYSIOTHERAPIST

In the seventies, I was working as a physiotherapist in Toronto. One day on my way to work, I saw a clear vision of an old radiant face of a man.

Since at the time I was studying basic psychology, I figured I was hallucinating. Yet, despite my attempts to stop thinking about it, it took hold of me like a vice-grip.

Six months later I stopped by the book-cellar on Yorkville in Toronto. There on the shelf, I saw the face of the man that had appeared to me, on the cover of a book. The book was titled "The Spiritual Teachings of Ramana Maharshi." It was a small, $1.95 book.

My body began to shake uncontrollably. I bought the book and read the whole 100 pages or so in one evening without sleeping that night. I went over it several times.

The next day I gave my resignation to my position. I retired to a basement apartment contemplating what had happened. I had saved enough money to live comfortably for a year or two.

However, as fate should have it, while performing Yoga postures to keep in shape outside the apartment on the lawn, I was approached by a YMCA scout who was looking for a Yoga teacher. I accepted the offer and after a year teaching as many as 12 classes a week in various places throughout the city, I was approached by CBC's *Food for Thought* for an interview. I was asked for a second interview due to growing interest in both Yoga and how thought affects mind and body.

A short TV series followed. During that time, I wrote a book titled, *Be Aware – Be Free*. I had a reasonable following and, having moved into a larger place, I started giving talks. This became the Unitrust Foundation, Uni-Trust meaning the trust in Unification or Oneness. After this, I travelled to Vancouver by car and also taught Yoga and meditation at the University of British Columbia.

CHAPTER THREE

27 YEARS LATER (AWAKENING)

It was in the year 2000 that I had my awakening. It happened during a conflicted relationship where I realized I didn't have an answer.

My partner had moved into my one-bedroom apartment after leaving her two sons, whom she sent to her former husband; her car, her dog and the house she owned. From Denver, Colorado, she gave up everything to be with me.

After a couple of months, the guilt of leaving everything behind took its toll and life became a catch-22. There was nothing I could do for her. I felt damned if I did anything and damned if I didn't.

In exasperation, I moved into the bathroom, closed the door and cried, "Please, Bhagavan help me!" Then it happened. There was a sudden shift where Burt disappeared, yet there was just this Light that "said," "There are no answers, but this moment."

There is only THIS! It swept away in a stroke all that I had been taught or come to believe. A realization that I am a human being; a BEING playing the human role of Burt. It is this that is now writing this book.

During that time, I was working as a hypnotherapist, and this awakening gently shifted it into another practice which became "Supersentience", a way to see directly into one's true Being.

This book follows this theme. You are a human being; a Being playing the human role. If you can intuitively grasp this simple message then your seeing will be clear.

CHAPTER FOUR

YOU ARE A HUMAN BEING

To make "you are a human being" clearer to grasp in its utter simplicity, please picture the following of Human and Being:

Visualize two wolves inside you. One is filled with fear, seeking itself in things and objects of the world; uncertain, insecure, angry, frightened, jealous, sorrowful. It is feeling a continual lack filled with unconscious guilt, lies, false sense of self called ego and ignorance of one's true nature.

Then picture another wolf. He is open, innocent, loving, peaceful, joyful, serene, relaxed, and emphatic. He listens within, in Being itself.

Now comes the million dollar question. Before you read further, reply to this question: "Which one wins?"

The answer is very simple. The one that wins is the one you feed!

When I get e-mail questions such as…

"Why do I often feel so bad?"

"Why do so many negative thoughts torment me?"

"Why do I often feel so awful and empty?"

The answer is simple. You are feeding the human while ignoring the Being. It is all about BEING. To ignore BEING is to be controlling, desiring to get your own way, selfish, demanding, angry, intolerant. In other words, feeling separate from Being!

BEING is the truth of you and it means simply **TO BE**! TO BE means to be here and now without past (which is gone anyway) and without future (which can never be here).

Why do we feed the human and forget the Being? Isn't it because we believe we are our past experiences, our conditioning?

It is true that we can't help identifying with the past, but one moment of honest looking and asking, "What am I right now?" will reveal that you are nothing but BEING. This is scary to the human because it wants to be "somebody." It wants to be special because it wants to be loved.

Here is the crux of the matter – BEING is LOVE itself and therefore, can never be experienced by the human who craves and needs love. LOVE is not "something." LOVE is the recognition that you are BEING itself…oneness with all…no separation whatsoever!

All there is, is this Being appearing as a human. And since you are a human being then you seem to live in duality.

Being is nothingness, known also as Spirit, and it appears as everything. Being is the absolute, appearing as the relative. Being is the emptiness we misinterpret, which in truth, is fullness. Being is the uncaused and timeless essence, yet appearing as the caused and humans. Being is Oneness appearing as separation.

Being is the real subject appearing as object. Thus the singular BEING appears as the plural "we" and "us" and "them". Being is impersonal, but appears as seeming personal while it inhabits a form…role-playing form. Being is regarded as the unknown and appears as the known.

These explanations of duality appear as if they are real knowledge, but they are words pointing to the wordless that your intuitive heart can "hear" when it awakens to listening.

Here's the punch line. There is nothing happening, but only seems to happen. All this you will understand through your intuitive heart when the "human being" in you is finally seen clearly. The hope of this book is to bring you to that seeing.

CHAPTER FIVE

Seeing is Greater than Understanding

Seeing is more than understanding; seeing is the essence of the Being in "you" finally listening to the truth.

Understanding is intellectual. Seeing is immediate and always NOW!

The human in us is always seeking the Being, but doesn't know it. Hopefully, by the end of this book, you will be able to intuit this seeing.

When my clarity emerged in the year 2000 in the bathroom, I could see "things" I never saw before, even though I played the part of spiritual teacher.

When I met a "person" there was the seeing that his/her consciousness was seeking itself through the words, speech, manners, body-language, enneagram type, and zodiac sign. Even the way he/she walked, expressed and moved all indicated how the search was taking place.

The search was and is an incessant seeking of Being without any awareness of it happening, thus, the "person" thought he/she was their own action.

There was also the seeing that there was no personal doer at all except as a conditioned response to the need for Being.

This daily, conditioned consciousness carried within, one feels an unconscious discomfort, a subtle feeling that something is missing and one is not complete. This creates a stress calling for completion, often resulting in moodiness, depression, anger, fear, doubt, frustration and the need for love through a relationship or bonding with someone. Of course, none of this was wrong since one had no choice.

However, seeing is deeper than this seeking. There is primarily the seeing that he/she is divine, a pure essence of Being already in the midst of its seeking.

You are a Being playing the role of human.

As you read this, keep in your awareness that you are a human being; **Being playing the human role**. In this Awareness, the possibility of an early seeing is possible because the intuitive heart is ever eager to see the truth.

Yet, paradoxically, our conditioned identity is frightened from this great Truth of Oneness. Thus, it spends its energy protecting, defending and maintaining its status quo through control, guilt and fear.

A Course in Miracles states that the greatest fear is the fear of waking up to the Truth of your Being. Therefore, it is logical to assume that **all emotional pain is really a defense against waking up.**

How do we do this? **We do it through escape.** So we can say that we are a human being – the human is an escapist and the Being is the lover.

CHAPTER SIX

The Escapist

I received the following e-mail this morning while writing this article.

"There is something inside of me that almost feels like a mean bully that doesn't let me completely enjoy life, it almost seems like another life-form that sort of taunts and tortures me or maybe it is the bully inside of me? I'd like to be 'all for me' and in love with myself! How do I release this?"

There were other e-mails that were similar complaints of negative thinking and how to control and get rid of them.

What do all these e-mails have in common? **They are describing the ESCAPIST called "me"**. It is the human part of us that has forgotten the Being and so tries to escape from facing its own creations.

When the human has forgotten about the BEING, which is LOVE, it tries to gain it through control. Control doesn't know how to deal with anything that confronts it except through trying to get rid of it, which means escape!

The human part of us is always looking for the Being, but doesn't know it. It does it by seeking it through this world of illusion. In other words, it is seeking itself through another or others.

This becomes an automatic ESCAPE from itself. For example, **the human seeks love by being loved**. This is an automatic escape from loving itself. The true Self (BEING) is the lover in us. Thus, by seeking love, we escape the lover, creating a contradiction of our natural state. Then we wonder why we suffer. Every time we seek love we are saying, "I am not love!"

The human is made up of three strong escapes:

1. The fear of facing the truth by escaping it. For example, **<u>we seek someone to love us</u>** because we lack love, yet we know we are escaping the truth. This subtle feeling is enough to create unconscious guilt. The feeling as if there's something wrong with us.

2. From inner guilt comes the need to control in order to escape further what we don't want to face. Control comes in three ways: Fear of being controlled; fear of losing control and the need to be constantly in control, ever afraid of losing it. This control makes us anxious, panicky and stressed out most of the time through the escape of facing the obvious. What is the obvious?

3. The obvious is that we keep choosing escape rather than love. For example, someone says something or does something like ignoring us or acts rudely and so on. We escape the situation by not looking at it as it actually is and so we turn it into a negative. Before we know what happened we are thinking negatively. This self-concern; self-pity; self-indulgence in negative thinking are all escapes from the moment.

The question is, "What are we escaping all the time from?"

CHAPTER SEVEN

THE KEY

Here's the key by answering the question, "I want to get rid of negative thinking and yet it keeps haunting me. Why is that?"

Do you know the obvious answer?

Negative thinking is your choice because it reinforces the belief that you are justified in defending and protecting yourself, thus escaping the fact that there is no such thing as "me" that needs to be protected and defended.

Escapes bring in their wake a frightening life filled with ruined relationships, dissatisfied situations, unfulfilling practices and a life filled with disappointments, regrets and guilt.

What are we escaping? **We are escaping the truth**. The Truth is LOVE known as Oneness, but we stress that we are a separate individual apart from Oneness.

This is why Jesus said in the *Course* that all emotional suffering is a defense against awakening. It is an escape from looking at the Truth, that there's no such thing as a personal identity but Oneness appearing as you. You are a human being; Being playing the human role.

CHAPTER EIGHT

WHAT BRINGS SUFFERING?

What brings so much suffering? **It is called unconscious guilt.** It is the continual feeling that there's something wrong with us; that we are missing something; that somehow we are missing the boat, and so desperately escape this feeling by indulging in self-pity and self-concern, believing this negativity to be real. We are escaping the simple Truth that there's no me at all and there never was. This truth is too much for the ego to bear.

We appear to live in a world inhabited by separate individuals who, to an extent, have free will and choice and the ability to take action which bring about consequences. This human belief is almost universally accepted without question simply because there is not yet awareness that you are BEING and merely playing the role of human.

For example, you are reading these words and it will definitely be your choice to either stop or continue reading…or so it seems. The truth is that if you are not ready to read this then you won't. The choice is not yours, it just seems to be.

It appears that your choice is directed towards the attainment of pleasure and the avoidance of pain. We strongly believe as humans that we can make our life work without recognizing that there is no such thing as "my life" but only Life. This is the principle that apparently motivates most personal and global activity. We never ask this most enlightening question, **"Who is it that lives?"**

The human part of us seems to live in a world that is threatening, thus we gather various groups and create sets of rules which bring some sort of order and protection. To follow, conflict and tension arise and our negotiations are not always successful. This is all the human seeking of the Being without actually knowing that the Being is the Reality and needs no conditions.

Most people seek a deeper meaning and purpose to life which can bring to the human part hope and comfort, exacerbating our very life to moods and even despair since following such concepts is impossible.

Being, on the other hand, is be-ing and not expecting anything to change, nor wanting anything to change. After all, there is no human self, as we thought, that can be controlled.

This deeper meaning drives us to some religion and the belief in a deity outside of us. These can be a sort of temporary respite from our unconscious guilt and pain of being human, but their limitation soon takes over and we find ourselves losing our faith.

It appears that our whole way of life is grounded on a fundamental belief which could only be seen as an assumption about reality.

As the Italian Founder of Psychosynthesis, Assagioli, wrote, "Ninety-five percent of our energy is spent protecting, defending and maintaining our self-image and it is all imagination, unreal." The belief in being human is so strong that we totally forget about the BEING.

The possibility of Oneness is frightening to the human because it lacks the personal touch which we feel we need. Therefore, due to this unconscious fear, we are blind to what is obvious, which is the timeless essence of this moment. After all, yesterday is history and gone. Tomorrow is just a concept that never arrives. There is only THIS moment without an EXIT. Intuitively we know this, yet our unconscious fears arise to combat this knowing.

CHAPTER NINE

Facing Our Biggest Fear

We try to justify our emotional pain to keep asserting our personal identity. The "knowing" that our personal identity is a fiction is horrifying, and so we continue holding on to the idea that emotional darkness is real so that we have some semblance of identity to hold on to.

This identity is known as ego, and if we were to give it a good intuitive "seeing", we would see how our resistance is driving us mad.

The solution is so simple and obvious that we don't even dare contemplate it. The solution is doing nothing, which is BEING.

Through this nothingness, we create a space, a respite and a chance to see beyond its mirage. It is here, in this non-doing, that we shift from human to Being.

CHAPTER TEN

BEING WITHOUT THE PERSONAL HUMAN?

Is it possible that our whole reality is BEING without the personal human, which means it is all a Unified Field of impersonal dynamic, devoid of all intention, direction or purpose? Just THIS alone?

The conditioned mind will get more than upset at such a possibility and will reject it out of fear, and our seeming suffering goes on.

Here's the wonderful news. When I saw clearly, that there was only this moment and no possible exit eternally, there was also no person to suffer and, as a result, a whole incredible energy emerged – an expression of vibrant passionate aliveness.

This possibility would overturn the belief and value upon which we base our behavior and would undermine that we have any choice about the behavior. Thus, we allow everything to happen and, in that allowing, where's the suffering? After all, there is no personal doer!

Is our cause and purpose simply a dream? After all, if there is nothing to get or gain, nothing to overcome or control or fix because it is all THIS moment forever eternally, then it would seem that awakening is a disaster. There would be no one left to run their lives and possibly no managing director of the universe to offer guidance. If our life is lost then everything is lost. But hold on a minute, is it really like that?

This is when awakening will show us that this nothingness we so feared is everything, and nothing is separate – a Heaven that cannot be imagined but yet can be lived.

CHAPTER ELEVEN

Experiencing the Futility of the Human

One of my Skype clients from Miami, deeply depressed over the death of her lover and loss in her family, was on the verge of committing suicide when she e-mailed me. Spiritual knowledge was not her experience, as she was primarily a career woman.

When I asked about her depression, she told me her story and I listened for about 10 minutes. When it was over I asked her about what depression was to her and she related information she read from psychology books.

After listening to her for yet another ten minutes or so I asked her how she felt in her depression.

Her reply was what I was waiting to hear; she said emphatically, **"I feel totally helpless!"**

Then I asked her, "This means that there's nothing you can do. You cannot fix it nor overcome it, right?"

She agreed.

"Then do absolutely nothing about it, not even wish it to go away. Helplessness is a state often reached by the human mind and any attempt to resist it can lead to emotional dysfunction."

She looked at me puzzled, "So what can I do?"

I pointed out how the human mind is forever hoping to control even itself. I also knew from her expression that further explanations would be useless and so I asked her to relax and enter the alpha state of mind through my suggestions as she relaxed in her chair.

When the hour was over, I gave her the homework of "feeling" this helplessness as if she was an unbiased observer of it. I made it clear not to think about it but feel it as it actually is.

Apparently, she did as suggested, because after two days, I received an e-mail from her that literally screamed with joy. She announced that her depression was gone totally and she had more energy than she ever had, even prior to her depression.

Two days later still she confirmed her energy as stable with an accompanying article of her state. Finally, she made up her mind that she'd go on a speaking tour regarding this "miracle healing."

Eckhart Tolle, who is the author of the bestselling book *The Power of Now*, was also on the verge of quitting life after prolonged depression.

He finally screamed, "I can't live with myself anymore."

At this point he realized, "Are there two of me – myself and I?"

It was this recognition of the futility of the human ego that made the birds sing the next day. He sat in quiet stillness after this experience, enjoying the bliss of Being. After a few years he wrote the bestselling book.

Why does the direct experience of helplessness bring a breakthrough? Actually, it is the state of recognizing the futility of the human ego that brings the great consciousness shift.

When we create enough space in meeting the helplessness without doing anything, then we automatically enter pure Being. It is this total allowing that shifts our human helplessness into the true state of Being.

The moment we see the "me" as a helpless and unreal part of us, then it falls away and what is left is our true nature. The recognition that your "me" is the very problem that caused all the emotional suffering, and yet in itself, is helpless to do anything or fix or attain anything, is itself the greatest gift.

You are seen as wholeness, without expectations or demands. Confusion and resistance dissolve in the light of openness and nothing will be left.

Paradoxically, it is when you are left utterly empty with nothing to hold on to that a breakthrough happens. Out of that nothingness emerges the indescribable fullness and wonder of simple Being.

After this breakthrough, it doesn't mean that there won't be any fear arising. It simply means that there will be no more "me" to identify with it. Therefore, you are totally free to be who you are.

The greatest richness is not wealth, success or accomplishment but the death of the "me" that will leave one free from bondage.

The profound simplicity of this seeing of the obvious is always one step too near for the mind and "understanding" to ever approach.

Herein lies the invitation to give the deductive analytical and conditioned mind a rest and simply breathe in these words in this book with the effortlessness and resonance from which they arose.

The human ego is incessantly seeking the Being and yet it is this very seeking that blocks the seeing. Why? Because seeking makes it seem like something you can attain, and attainment gives one the belief that it is not the case at the moment.

You are already a human being and there's nothing to attain, to accomplish nor fix, but simply see the truth of this moment as it is.

CHAPTER TWELVE

The Glory of Nothingness!

The human part of us is frightened of nothingness, and that goes with wanting to do something about it. The greatest known teaching is non-dualism, which means there is no separation from our natural Oneness nature.

Any personal attempt to "do" something about your situation (which is experienced emotionally as a problem) causes all the known human suffering.

A Course in Miracles states emphatically "you need do nothing," for in that non-doing and allowing, another force (Oneness) takes over and we are led to what is needed at that moment.

Our true nature is BEING, and this means "to be." Therefore, what is called God is LOVE itself. Through our non-doing but trusting God (let go and let God), we are led automatically into the right action that serves us the best.

What is called "nothingness" is really no-thing-ness referring to the essential spirit nature. Nothingness is the essence of Life and is not existing per se, but that which produced existence out of itself like a spider weaving a web from itself.

GOD IS!

No two words can give more power, truth and glory than those two words. If they were to be realized, even minutely, in their true meaning, then what follows is a transformation.

CHAPTER THIRTEEN

Be Still and Know I AM God

Be still for a moment and allow yourself to "see" that THIS very moment is not subject to past and future. The past is gone, although our reference to self is always about our name, position, accomplishment and conditioning.

At this moment, see how asking "Who am I?" will reveal no answer. Why? Because in this stillness there is no "you" to answer anything, since you cannot refer to the past and neither the future.

As you continue knowing that there is no "knowing" who you are, see that this moment has no exit ever. In fact, **you are sitting in the timeless essence of reality.** "You" is a spaciousness, an open field of pure Awareness.

There was never a beginning nor is there an end to this moment. It is impossible to grasp by the mind; however, you can "see" by your intuitive knowing, that this MOMENT never started or could end. FEEL IT!

It is Being this, within, which recognition happens. Remember that the mind is only a storyteller and can't possibly comprehend timelessness. When sitting still beyond any story, just watching IS-ness of now, the intuitive heart will start to feel the essence of Being without words or labels.

The whole process of waking up from our sleep is through seeing our timeless nature and the futility of the human state that is totally powerless.

Awakening cannot be brought about because there is no one to do it. It happens when the timeless nature is glimpsed through seeing the invalidity of the personal ego.

Paradoxically, we see something that sounds rather confusing and it is this – when awakening happens, there is also the seeing that nothing actually happened except you see clearly there is no "you" other than awareness of this moment.

In fact, there is no such thing as awakening or liberation. The fact that awakening happened proves there was no awakening but rather, Oneness always being the case. In other words, you finally see what is true – all there is, is THIS moment!

PART II

CHAPTER FOURTEEN

Is There Really a Secret?

I have been depressed and clearly saw my helplessness, but it didn't help me over the depression?

There was still the need to be in control and get rid of the depression, thereby missing the point of seeing that the ego is totally helpless to do anything. It is in this total seeing of helplessness that the human shifts into Being.

If there's no purpose, no choice, no destiny then what's left?

When we identify with the human ego, as most people do initially, then it seems there is reincarnation, karma, choices, destiny, purpose and somewhere to go to. This is known in new-age circles as the "journey" of the soul.

When awakening happens, we see clearly that there is no longer movement of mind simply because our whole focus is the BEING. Be-ing just IS and has no action other than being Home – our true identity as Oneness.

This does not mean that there is no mind/body function anymore. It simply means that we see things as they are. Thoughts are thoughts that come and go; emotions are emotions that come and go; body recycles from infant to adulthood, but the Oneness, which is BEING, does and IS everything and we rest in that.

In this rest there is security, freedom, safety, joy and fulfillment. Actions that spring forward are seen as Oneness acting through us and everything is OKAY! This is known as the peace that passeth understanding.

The human is motivated by seeking the Being, but it doesn't know it. When there are glimpses of it, then the conditioned mind becomes motivated towards awakening (which never happens because in truth there is no future).

Finally, a strong drive becomes evident for our true Home, and awakening happens through grace.

With awakening and seeing clearly emerge also a deep rest, a freedom that is hard to describe, and all seeking stops dead. The seeking to improve, to achieve or attain something, to accomplish some practice, to go somewhere, is completely dropped without anyone doing the dropping.

This awakening is itself unconditional love.

Please see videos at www.youtube.com/burtharding/ and www.youtu.be/yZo7EAmzBoo.

How does* The Secret *that was made into a movie fit in?

The Secret was a great success because the producers were wise to its attraction. It pulled in millions of viewers because the Law of Attraction was turned into attainment, accomplishment, abundance and everything that the ego seeks and craves for.

The Law of Attraction states simply: "You become and attract what you focus on." The homeless person is a perfect example of the outcome from the Law of Attraction. He/she attracted what they focused on in their mind.

According to studies, the majority of those who bought the *Course* or the book, *The Secret,* never attained what they hoped, with only about 5% succeeding.

The Law is not at fault at all. It states that you become what you think about most of the time. You are your Living-Question.

The real "secret" which is hiding in plain sight is BEING. You are already a BEING playing the human role but somehow so identified with being a personal separated individual that you don't see what is obvious.

Please watch video titled #31 "The Real Secret" at www.youtu.be/pNQ1pgbpaYU.

CHAPTER FIFTEEN

THE HIGHEST TEACHING

Lately a lot has been emphasized in non-duality as the highest teaching. What makes it the highest teaching?

You are a human being, a Being playing the human role. BEING is the highest teaching and it is non-dualistic. When you just "BE" with whatever is, which means there is absence of self, then there is both unconditional love and freedom of Being.

Being is obvious and is hiding in plain sight. The Fall of mankind has been known as the sin of separation. Separation means that you believe, without question, that you are just a human and separate from "out there."

Being is all there is and if we just sit still (without thinking) for a moment, we will see that we don't even know who we are. All we know is that we are here.

If you listen completely to what is being said here, you can have a glimpse of Being. It is so simple that the mind won't believe nor accept it. To actually "hear" these words right now is already quite a step beyond its hiding and it is revolutionary. It is all about the rediscovery of who it is that lives. And it is Being that lives.

Without Being, what you call "my body" would be just dust. There is only Being and there is no one who is separate, even as you read these words.

Please hear them instead of just reading them. There is no separate one. There is NO ONE who can be separate. It is all one consciousness.

The conditioned mind will rebel at this stillness and say, "Stop! I am a person and I feel separate. I am an individual and my mother and my father and the people and teachers and bosses and wives and husbands are all telling me that I am a separate person who can make choices for better or worse."

This is how the dream of the conditioned mind is created.

You are convinced that this is your life and even though you see life around you, you still equate the life that is lived as a separate individual. However, as you look and SEE that in this stillness there is only NOW, so where is this life of yours apart from NOW?

If your conditioned mind convinces you that you are separate, then you'll emerge from this stillness still "not seeing" and go about searching for that elusive Being somewhere else, calling it something else according to your religious, philosophical belief.

Non-duality is the highest teaching because it is focused on what is unchanging and eternal; it is beyond the duality of human and Being… It is Being alone. It is the Being that plays the role of human. Do you get it now?

Is* A Course in Miracles *a non-dualistic teaching?

It definitely is! In fact, it is a teaching that very few people understand its true message. The message of the *Course* is based on one factor only, namely, forgiveness!

It is not forgiveness in the conventional sense. It is forgiveness that transcends the belief in doing anything wrong. It is SEEING that there is ultimately nothing to forgive because there is only Christ. Christ means Being.

When your true nature is glimpsed as this eternal moment, then the *Course*, in its workbook, has done its job and the study of it is no longer needed.

The *Course* is a self-study course. It has 365 lessons, one a day for a full year. It trains the conditioned mind to eventually see only Spirit even when it sees the material world.

Experiencing the teaching, there are glimpses of transcendence of time and space. It brings you closer to Oneness than another course can.

Many who study the *Course* do not understand its main message of compassion and forgiveness. The mind takes over because they do not practice the daily lessons. Most students do not practice the workbook, preaching it instead of forgiving themselves.

Forgiveness is another word for letting-go, surrendering, allowing, doing nothing and Being. The *Course* even states "you need do nothing" which alone, during a difficult mind-game of emotional pain, can lead to Being (as already discussed).

So many people belong to some religion or are conditioned by one. What is religion anyway?

The human longs for structure and something to believe in. It is the nature of the mind to organize truth. The original Founders of the major religions were realized Beings, but their followers organized it.

One time, a Yogi was walking along and he met the devil. The Yogi said to the devil, "You are not going to be pleased because Truth is lying on the road ahead and people will find it!"

The devil smiled and said, "Wonderful!"

The Yogi was surprised. "What do you mean wonderful, after all, Truth will annihilate you!"

The devil still looked contented. "Wait and see what people will do when they find this truth lying there!"

And they both watched. They witnessed people picking up the truth and putting it in their pocket as a possession.

Then the devil said, "You see, they already own it and start fighting among themselves after they organize it."

This organization of truth with ritual, and so on, can't be helped because the conditioned human mind does not know another way. When awakening happens, conventional religion merely drops.

Can you explain 'Being' in simpler terms such as in daily life?

Being does not know daily life, but only LIFE itself. The word "daily" refers to time-consciousness; when the earth faces the sun it is called day and when it is away from the sun we call it night and time for rest.

These are unending cycles for the human form to survive. What we call daily life is simply a repetition of actions habituated by conditioned mind. We get up, have breakfast, go to work, come home, watch TV or talk to wife or husband then go to sleep and get up again with the same cycle.

Daily life is a circle like the clock that starts with 12 noon and ends with midnight, starting over again and again. The earth rotates around the sun and creates the semblance of time known as daily life, days, weeks, months and years, and they create biological change such as the recycling of the body, which we think we are.

Cycles create chronological time such as the calendar, and also create ego time known as psychological time, where we believe that there is such a thing as past or future.

When we become still and stop using the daily mind for a moment, we will see that all there is, is THIS moment for always, never-ending without an exit ever.

When we see the above as obvious, which it certainly is, then we start living from Being. There is only Being. It seems to be hiding but it is also in plain sight.

Why is it that everyone I know misses the Being?

You are a human being, a Being playing the human role, but here's the trick – you don't know it because the mind (including the brain) is linear, in order to help us live daily life and survive in our conditioned way.

Linear means that events follow each other in progressive succession. In other words, there seems to be a sequential order of events. Upon waking up we see this "game" very clearly, that no such thing is happening but only in our imaginative viewpoint.

There is only Being, which is the NOW moment forever appearing as if it is moving into some phantom future, but it is always NOW!

Listen carefully! You are a human being; this means that you are a BEING playing the role of human. Once you grasp this intuitive knowing, all questions will be solved!

Can you explain what blocks most people from seeing the truth and living from it?

You are a human being; a Being playing the human role. The reason you do not see this clearly yet is because the conditioned person you think you are (the ego) protects you from anything that threatens itself. Essentially, it will do its best to keep you safe, secure and protected.

Here's an example of this protection. I used to love dancing on Saturday nights. Everyone would be seated waiting for the band to start playing and having a beer or a drink. The ballroom in the center is open and free, waiting for couples to start dancing. What I noticed was the reluctance to be first on the dance floor. Why?

In a way, this is the protection of the ego against being exposed and feeling unsafe and insecure. The paradox, that practically no one was aware of, is that this protection is itself insecurity and lack of safety.

The ego will do anything to protect itself from exposure. When it is aggressive, then it demands attention, love and respect. Anger arises if such threat is experienced. The threat is often perceived by the constant fear of being exposed.

Thus, the ego harbors continual unconscious feelings of guilt as if one is not good enough or there is something wrong, brought about by the nature of inner knowing that something is missing and feels incomplete.

And what is this feeling of incompletion? What seems to be missing? Isn't it that you are not really a person, but wholeness itself expressed in Being? You are a Being playing the role of human but do not know it due to a conditioned past.

This is the dream everyone is in. The dream of being a person (ego), known as a separate individual called "me." It is the great deception also known as original sin in some teachings. It is the fundamental Fall of man; a feeling of separation from Wholeness (Oneness).

Whilst we remain locked within the apparent experience of being a separate individual living in an existence with which we have to negotiate, we live in a state of dreaming, sometimes even a nightmare.

In this dream-state, all that we do is governed by the law of opposites in which every so-called positive act is exactly and equally balanced by its opposite.

Therefore, all our personal attempts to make our life work, to reach some sort of perfection or to attain personal growth or freedom, are neutralized.

We discover, through deep reflection and understanding that as long as we continue in this dream we are, in reality, living in a circle. This circle will bring frequent feelings of depression, moodiness, frustration, fear, guilt, shame and anger at our predicament. We never ask, "Who is it that lives?"

Our nature is Oneness known as Being. It is this pure Awareness known as Presence, that which lives. It is the internal detached witness of everything that goes on while the conditioned ego will judge and blame and create havoc.

Our first and most important step is being aware of who it is that lives. We don't have a life of our own, and so saying "my life" is a misnomer. There is only Life.

CHAPTER SIXTEEN

The Lessons of Negative Emotion

How do we start seeing this?

We start by inviting every negative emotion as a lesson to learn from. We "learn" by seeing that there's nothing, as a person, we can do to control, fix or overcome a depression, anger, fear, worry, frustration, confusion or any negative emotion. As a person we are helpless to do anything.

Any attempt to overcome or fix this so-called problem will end in a much worse condition. The insane asylums are filled with people who have resisted their emotions.

The first step is, therefore, NOT to resist at all, in fact do absolutely nothing, not even wishing it to go away. This puts the egoic person on the spot. The person (personal ego) wants to do something about it, and this is where most fail.

Also, this is where success is possible, if we just SEE (look) into it without any desire to do anything. It is this that makes the difference. By looking directly, unbiased and detached, into the emotion, there is BEING "activated." And, as you know, BEING is love itself. It is this love known as self-compassion that turns things around.

Remember this: Through allowing BEING to be with what is, no matter how seemingly painful, comes the discovery that the dream we are living has absolutely no purpose other than our awakening from it.

You often mention enneagrams in your sessions. Aren't these enneagrams part of the dream of being human?

Yes definitely! The enneagram type merely points out what is not real in a person; however, it is what the person feels, believes and experiences that creates the great block to awakening. These enneagrams point what the person (ego) believes to be real about them.

It was a great discovery by the Sufis, maybe a thousand years ago, and brought to the West by such great Masters like the Russian sage, Gurdjieff. Such enneagrams are also being studied at universities.

The point to keep in mind is that there is only ONE EGO and it has its own characteristics so that every man and woman that believes they are a person exhibits these characteristics.

The drive of the ego is to be separate and individual. It is incapable of love or warmth. It is selfish, greedy, fearful and unforgiving. It wants to get its own way at all costs. It seeks constantly for love and needs approval and justification for what it does. It has no ability to look at itself.

Many spiritual seekers who say, "I want to get rid of the ego," are simply playing the ego game of wanting to get rid of itself, which is impossible. The best way to rise above the ego-person is to laugh at its antics. Genuine laughter is something that the ego is incapable of.

Now the ego has one strong drive and that is to feel important, superior, separate and commanding attention. It starts as children, riding the bicycle shouting, "Look ma, no hands!"

The personal idea starts innocently enough and gathers speed with time, making life more difficult to live. Nowadays, the suicide rate is staggering. This drive for love, while incapable of truly loving, is ego's greatest search.

People are always seeking for attention, approval, relationships, importance and success. This drive is accepted as "normal." When the book *The Secret* came out as a movie, it literally swept the country. Why?

The movie pointed out a law of mind that can manifest anything, known as the Law of Attraction. Everyone's ego was perked by the promise of achievement and personal accomplishment. However, "the secret" was fully exposed in its true meaning. The Law of Attraction states simply, "You become what you focus on."

Here's an example of this focus. A woman complained about her mother driving her crazy with her bickering, complaining, negative comments and demeaning attitude. This woman could not forgive her mother at all, and she was enraged at even the idea of having to forgive her.

Months later, I heard from her again saying that now she is sick and having to spend Xmas holidays with her mother, and the very thought of it made her sick.

I mentioned forgiveness again but she wouldn't hear of it. Then we had a Skype session where I pointed out that the focus of her hate on her mother has turned her into her mother herself.

This shocked her, and she realized how alike she is to her mother. Of course she was becoming like her mother. After all, that was what she focused on. This was a typical Law of Attraction. We become what we focus on.

However, this story had a happy ending as this woman realized what was happening and took this lesson as an invitation. She forgave her mother and now she is happy in a new relationship with lots of love.

Where does the enneagram come in? There are nine different soul-types that all have one single drive, unconsciously of course, and that is to go Home (to the true Being nature, Oneness). This drive is a different need for each type, and it is this need, when seen, that will bring us Home to LOVE. Here are the nine needs:

1. **Need for perfection which often creates dissatisfaction.**
2. **Need for love which leads to low self-esteem.**
3. **Need for achievement which leads to lack of Being.**
4. **Need for identity justification which leads to feeling overwhelmed.**
5. **Need for feeling smart which leads to aloneness.**
6. **Need for safety and security which leads to fear of the world.**
7. **Need for future planning which leads to escape from now.**
8. **Need for control which leads to aggressive behavior.**
9. **Need for harmony which leads to fear of making waves.**

By knowing the fixation of our seeking, we can see the block of separation from Wholeness. It is this "seeing" alone that is necessary. That is, seeing exactly the contradiction of what we truly want.

So many counselors and psychologists suggest loving who we are, just as we are, is that helpful?

It is a step in the right direction for most people who are unaware of their true nature. Once we start seeing that we are okay as we are, then we can go deeper into the truth that there's no one to accept nor a self to love.

However, all true seeing is a "readiness" for it. The paradox is this – the moment we discover who it is that lives us, we also become clear that unconditional love is the whole point. It is in seeing there is no personal self that true love awakens.

Now picture the time when you fell in love. In those first moments, was there a self? Of course not! It is the absence of self that awakens lasting love.

How can one experience pure Being and still experience human needs?

As long as we are human, we remain human, but the focus shifts when awakening happens. Initially we are so caught in our conditioned ego that we are like robots and totally unconscious of our reactions and emotional feelings.

When awakening happens, there is only the shift from being human to Being Divine essence, and that's all. The capacity to love and enjoy is much greater and there is the awakening of wonder and inner passion for truth. But the human needs for dessert, for coffee, for making love, for enjoying a movie might still be there and enjoyed without guilt or personal concern, which has by now dropped off.

We enjoy life the same way we did before, but this time we are less inhibited, with no worry or self-concern, but simply free. The greatest gift is the freedom.

You keep saying human being. I understand the word human but somehow the term "Being" escapes me. What does the word Being mean?

Your true nature is BEING and not an ego. Whether you realize it or not, it is already the case. Knowing means there is nothing to worry about, nothing to fix, nothing to attain or accomplish.

Bei-ing simply means "to be" without attempting to change anything or control anything, and to simply allow BEING to act through you.

Did you know that from such ease and comfort come genius, real creativity and true accomplishment – not by us but ***through*** us?

There is just happening. All there is, is this happening. Nobody can teach you to be alive and breathe and eat and walk, talk and move your arms.

Who would have the arrogance to teach you to be, when there is only Being? Who would have the arrogance to say you have to change?

When you allow yourself to be with the knowing that BEING does everything through you, a whole new world will open up for you. What can fall apart through allowing Being is the idea that there is such a thing as an individual person.

When awakening happens, there is the clear seeing that no one ever did anything or accomplished anything – it was always Being working through the mind/body organism.

One evening during satsang I became a total witness to the fact that here was this form waving its arms and issuing forth sounding words in a chair, while others stared speechless. It was later that Burt came back noticing himself being acted.

All this might sound strange to someone reading it for the first time, but then it is the conditioned mind that is surprised and not that which lives the form.

Being is love, and oneness acts through it when there is the seeing that Being is all there is. When the human doesn't understand this, he/she becomes self-conscious, and then everything that comes through the form-body is an expression of conditioned beliefs filled with stress, fear, uncertainty and expectations. Our greatest gift and freedom and great joy emerge when there is absence of self.

What is the difference between understanding, seeing and intuitively knowing, and who's doing it?

You are a human being; a Being playing the human role. The human role is just memory conditioned into body-cells. It is the Spirit that makes the body look alive.

When we identify with the memory, which most people initially do, then understanding doesn't come easily and it is mostly intellectual interpretation.

When we begin to "feel" with our Awareness, so that we are filled with wonder at the magic of manifestation, then our intuitive heart opens. This opening brings sensitivity and compassion leading to deeper seeing. It is this deeper seeing that awakens us to the truth. This seeing has nothing to do with the human part of us.

CHAPTER SEVENTEEN

The Big Bang

How did all this manifestation start?

According to the teaching of *A Course in Miracles* and ancient teachings of the East, initially there was only Oneness. A heavenly state of Being where only God existed.

This was a joyous paradise that the mind cannot begin to grasp. There was no beginning and no end because time didn't exist in this eternal Beingness.

Then God created, out of Itself, another extension called Christ. God and Christ were equal in all respects; however, the Christ was an extension of its unconditional love to spread itself.

In this Oneness, there crept a tiny mad idea (as the *Course* phrases it), where the question arose for a millisecond, "What if I could experience playing by myself?"

This was like giving a match to a child who burned his parents' house down. From this mad idea, known as the Fall of Man or the banishment from the Garden of Eden, was created the Big Bang. It was the beginning of time and creation of mind.

From this universal mind emerged manifestation, where thought (mind) created the world and the human form. This was also the birth of duality, where Oneness became seeming split. Thus the human being was born.

In the first stages of its human evolution there was no understanding and very little awareness except of its surroundings and the instinct to survive. As the human began to become aware of its own Being, ever so slightly, accordingly its evolution began.

However, the point to be made clear is that all this manifestation is a dream of the mind, and never was and never can be real.

Can you explain the two aspects of Awareness, which is our true nature?

Awareness, which is timeless and therefore beyond birth and death, is who we truly are. Since the conditioned mind cannot grasp the timeless, then the word "awareness" is experienced as a blah concept.

As we expand in our "seeing", then we start to recognize that Awareness IS everything. The two aspects of Awareness are – Self-recognizing and Self-organizing. These two aspects cover the whole spectrum of reality.

Self-recognizing is quite direct. For example, ask anyone, "How do you know you exist?"

Then they'll say, "Of course I know I exist!"

Pursue that first question with, "Well how do you know?"

They will reply, "Because I am aware I exist."

From this you have two forms of knowing. One is that Awareness recognizes itself, and secondly that without it there is no existence, period.

Now Self-organizing is the heart of the matter, and once we fully recognize it, we start feeling the power of the true Self and how we are taken care of. How IT does everything, and more importantly, how our need for safety and security is an indirect search for the Pure Awareness that we are.

Initially, we are so materially bound that Awareness is in the background, and we wonder why we suffer. For example, our human need for security and safety emerges from our true nature, which is safe and secure. Because the human identifies with the material illusion called world, then he/she feels that money will bring security, and a love affair will bring safety, such as a home and comforts and protection. This is part of the illusory dream of the human ego and creates untold suffering. Why? Simply because human safety and security are impossible.

Self-organizing is "seen" when we become still and observe life around us. For example, did you ever ask how a simple fetus from the seed of a man creates kidneys, eyes, blood, flesh, brain, liver and the human form as we know it? Who is the director of such a creation? Who directs such a fetus to become a human form? It is the Self-organizing principle of pure Awareness.

Another example is the perfection of the earth's movement around the sun, creating the semblance of time in a chronological, biological and even psychological form.

When we start to awaken to the power and glory of Self-Awareness, we will also begin to see the utter stupidity of the ego and its illusion. The ego is the opposite of what is true and abiding, and its whole nature is suffering and fear from the idea that human beings are separate from God (Source).

What is the difference between consciousness and Awareness?

The two work together and are regarded as one. However, consciousness emerged from Awareness and started the concept of time and even the idea of separation.

Consciousness came about when the human became conscious of itself. (Please remember that I am talking about consciousness and NOT Pure Consciousness which Bhagavan Ramana Maharshi quoted as Awareness itself.)

The intelligence started when Awareness became aware of its own consciousness. Yet both consciousness and Awareness are ever-lasting.

Consciousness is Mind. Consciousness contains thought, emotions, and also helps the human to wake up when he/she becomes aware of its own consciousness and begins to see the bigger picture of awareness itself.

What happens to our beliefs, which all humans cherish, when we realize that the "me" is just a concept of separation?

When we start "seeing" that all the world is imagination (mind), then we also "see" that our human forms, which we take so seriously as whom we are, are seen as a self-image. We expand beyond imagination (consciousness) into pure Awareness or pure Being.

At this point all beliefs just drop, and in their place comes a "knowing" beyond concepts.

I keep hearing that the universe is holographic, what does that mean?

Holographic, in simple terms, means Oneness. Every fragment that seems separate from the rest is also the Oneness. For example, a simple wave of the ocean is still the whole ocean because it is the same water.

Every single human being is a Being and the Whole itself. Nothing is separate from anything else. All is interdependent, interrelated and interconnected.

When a human being feels lonely and alone, then he/she is in what is known as total unawareness of their true nature. When he/she starts feeling the connection with All-That-Is, then loneliness is impossible. Through the awakening of seeing everything as holographic is also seen that the smallest fragment is still the Whole.

Are human needs emerging from Being?

YES! Everything emerges from Being since there is only Being. Being shows us what is beautiful and loving and open and freeing and fulfilling. However, when it is received by the "person" who believes he is just a human ego, then the interpretation becomes a need rather than what already IS the case.

Here's an example. The Being let's you know intuitively that safety and security are your birthright as a Being of Light. This good news is received as a NEED for it because the belief in the human ego is that one is flawed.

Seeing yourself as an ego, then the perception of security becomes insecurity, and safety becomes lack of safety. We have turned LOVE into a NEED for it. This has to be seen clearly.

All of your needs are what you want most. The reason you want them is because they are already fulfilled in your heart. In fact, if you were asked, "How would you prefer to feel right now?" you would reply, "To feel whole."

So you see, your preference for wholeness means that wholeness is your birthright, but the ego turns it around into, "How I wish I was whole!"

The ego always feels not good enough, and so interprets everything in its limited form and does not receive the message as it actually was meant.

CHAPTER EIGHTEEN

WHO IS IN CONTROL?

In the book, as well as the movie,* The Secret, *one is told to control what one wants. My question is: How do we allow and accept that we have no control as a human and yet focus our minds on what we want in order to create it?

This is a common question and many seekers are baffled by it after seeing *The Secret* movie and book. First of all, you are a human being, a Being playing the human role. Once you begin to glimpse this, you'll also start "seeing" that everything you need is already in your true nature.

Since you have interpreted safety and security as NEEDS rather than who you are, then you have created a feeling of lack. This LACK is typical of the ego-person. And this is why the hype in *The Secret* movie was so attractive to the average viewer.

For example, an insecure person would think, "If I can make a lot of money, then I can do what I want, when I want, and be free!"

The problem is that this need, which was interpreted by the ego, has become a strong desire consciously. This conscious desire for riches is held back by the belief in the subconscious that one does not deserve it or doesn't feel the strong motivation for it. The result is failure!

The people who became rich through the Law of Attraction did so because they were meant for it and were motivated towards it. Here's another fact most people are not aware of. Since you are a Being playing the role of John or Mary, you are already (as a Being) fulfilled but have interpreted this feeling as, "How I wish I would feel abundant…"

Also, the script has already been written. In other words, if you were meant to be rich you would feel motivated for it whether you saw the *Secret* movie or not.

Our desires for wealth, success, money and prestige are the result of believing we lack something and that the world is real, instead of the imagination from the mind. The moment we start understanding the personal ego and forgive it, the sooner we start truly living in freedom and abundance.

All the hype of *The Secret* movie was towards getting people hooked into buying it. The Law of Attraction definitely works, and unless we are attuned to it as our true nature, we shall draw to us all the beliefs we have accumulated and help them to manifest.

A man came to see me once regarding this "secret" and why it didn't work for him. He said that he took a course on it, read the book and saw the movie several times, but he failed miserably to be a success in his business.

I had him lie down to be put under deep relaxation to discover the subconscious content regarding his continual failure. He recalled how, as a young child, he often felt awkward, being yelled at by his father telling him, "You'll never amount to anything, you're such a klutz."

Therefore, what manifested through the Law of Attraction were these words of his father.

The ego person has no control over "his life" simply because he has no life…there is only LIFE, period. He is a BEING playing the human role of that man. He would have transcended this conditioning if he had forgiven his father and his remarks that dug deep.

How do we forgive if we are neither doers nor controllers?

That's why forgiveness is so powerful and life-changing, because it is not a "doing" but a "seeing." Suppose someone says something that hurts your ego (all psychological suffering is ego). You see clearly that nothing actually happened except that you believed those words.

By seeing words are nothing but a sound ushering forth from the mouth, you realize they hurt because you gave meaning to words that you believed about yourself. And seeing this absurd situation clearly, that nothing happened except some words that also mean nothing – then that's forgiveness.

My mind is often so busy often presenting negative thoughts. How can I stop this?

Have you ever tried stopping it? The very attempt at stopping it causes it to increase its impact and its repetition. So what do you do? Why do you need to do anything?

Thoughts are nothing unless we make them real in our unawareness. Thoughts are thoughts, so what? The moment you see thoughts as thoughts and have nothing to do with you, then you're free.

I often feel confused and unhappy for no apparent reason, why is that?

You have created this through some image you have about yourself. All images are just imagination and have no validity or importance in Truth. Therefore, next time you feel unhappy, stop and look at it – try to find where it is!

This looking by itself will dissolve it, for nothing is ever happening except our conditioned mind planting some idea how things should be. You are a Being playing the human role and it's wonderful. Just play!

I have just read your comments on* The Secret *movie. Can you speak further about the dynamics behind it and why it became so popular?

The greatest drawing card for people is when they know that they can get security and safety in a world they don't understand. *The Secret* movie was a great selling factor to people's basic needs.

For example, many so-called spiritual seekers do not want truth, which would mean the death of their ego, but want to be happy, at peace, secure, safe and fulfilled in a personal way. This basic need of the spiritual seeker never reaches fruition because it is not possible.

The key to the awakened life is the realization that one is not who they think they are at all. They are a BEING playing the human role, but at the same time, they have no idea of it.

Secondly, when they watch a movie such as *The Secret*, it excites their imagination that they can get what they want. The problem is that they think they want wealth, but what they really want is the means and freedom to do as they please.

If one really knows what they truly want, then they already have it. Why? Because the Law of Attraction, which is considered "the secret," states you can get what you want. However, there was a slight deception in that definition when it was advertised. The real definition of the Law of Attraction is this: ***You become what you imagine.***

Since the mind is mental pictures known as imagination and thoughts, this Law of Attraction is the law of mind. A perfect example of this law is the street person living as a bum; he got what he imagined.

I had so many clients complaining that they didn't get what they wanted. Upon investigation of what they focused on, were these subtle messages in the subconscious mind…

"I don't feel good enough."

"I feel I am missing something."

"There must be something wrong with me."

"I don't feel I deserve the best life has to offer."

Those messages were the images and thoughts that created the life they led.

The Law of Attraction never fails and is based on imagination. In fact, the whole world is a manifestation of imagination. Can you think of anything in the world that was not produced by the mind's imagination?

The moment you take imagination (what you imagine yourself to be) seriously, then it becomes your cross. The reason we are all deceived is because we live from our self-image believing we are a personal individual who is separate from others. This belief is man's greatest blunder, known as the "Fall" of man.

Another factor to consider is that *The Secret* was coined to fool the public into thinking and believing they are discovering "the secret." The **real secret** is not mind, but the BEING that produced mind out of itself. The truth is that every human is a Being playing the human role. Every human being is potentially a vast Being.

The reason this discovery of "who it is that lives" is so hard to come by is because the ego-human is conditioned to survive at all costs. It initially has no clue that it is only through "losing" the person that the true life is recognized and realized.

Jesus said, ***"When you lose yourself, you find yourself."***

Therefore, BEING is the greatest secret, but then it scares most unaware people and so it won't be a great selling point, will it? The ego enjoys being deceived because it is led by its imagination.

Imagination is the greatest drawing card, and shrewd businessmen know how to use it in their sales approach. For example, why is pornography now netting close to a billion dollars annually? The reason is simple enough – sex is 100% imagination.

While logic says, one plus one equals two, our intuitive heart, which is beyond logic, states one plus one equals ONE. How? Life without love is no life at all. Oneness is LOVE, unconditional love. Therefore, with one plus one, add love, the answer is still One. Oneness is what it is all about.

The *Course* says that that which is all-encompassing has no opposite. When two seeming opposites are joined they become ONE. Example, front and back are opposites but need each other because they complete each other. The opposite sides of a coin still make one coin. Up and down complete each other.

Oneness takes love *and* fear as One. How? Simply because fear is really a frustration of love and when added to love, it melts into greater love. Oneness joins opposites without seeing them as opposites, but complementary.

Everything comes from Being, but it is the way that the human interprets it that causes the misunderstanding or misconception. Where does the feeling of insecurity and lack of safety so rampant in the human ego emerge from?

Take a good look now and see where such NEEDS emerge from. They emerge from BEING, everything comes from BEING. BEING is all there is. Being is Oneness and therefore the only "thing" that is safe, secure, peaceful, happy, joyous and fulfilled.

This Oneness defined as BEING filters through into the human, the human who believes they are a limited self-image and knows themselves as a separate person. Therefore, when the BEING, which is wholly secure and safe, filters its fullness into the human, the human, feeling separate and isolated, interprets the security as insecurity. Why? Because the fullness seen in its limited image turns into a NEED instead of its fullness of Being.

This is why the human always carries the feeling of lack, which is expressed as NEED. Yet the intuitive heart (Holy Spirit) is ever guiding the human, if he but listens. No matter how deprived a human feels, yet if he asks from his own heart, "What do I really prefer to feel instead of this stress?"

Immediately, the heart would respond, "to feel whole." The human mind interprets this as a NEED rather than a fact of Being.

CHAPTER NINETEEN

SPIRITUAL FASCINATION

I was wondering why so many people are attracted to spiritual fascination rather than the Truth. For example, fascination such as Angels, channeling, talking to the dead, mediumship, ascended masters, reincarnation, karma, chakras, various techniques and methods to enhance supernatural powers and so on. Are these necessary or are they invalid as truth?

Truth is this: You are a human being, a Being playing the human role. The human role contains all facets of a journey that don't exist because all is ONEness. Initially all humans, who are not in touch with Being, believe that there's a journey going someplace, to some destination; believe that there's something to get, accomplish or to overcome and fix.

Fascination has two aspects to it. First, it gives us the feeling we are going to achieve our goal, and secondly, it also keeps us from losing our ego. This fascination has some validity, but often unseen.

Many aspects of "happenings" are the manifestation of the Holy Spirit, to give us greater impetus when we are ready for it. In my case, Baghavan Ramana Maharshi was a very real image. But it wasn't Ramana that appeared to me but the Holy Spirit, taking on that form to show me my next step in life.

There have been many sightings around the world of the Mother Mary. Many people were witnesses of this case and yet it was the Holy Spirit that took that form to get people "ready."

Gary Renard, in his famous bestselling book, which has been translated into over 20 different languages, had two ascended masters appear to him with the names of Arten and Pursah. Yet they were but the appearance of the Holy Spirit, to bring in greater awareness of the teaching of Jesus in *A Course in Miracles*.

All the different modes of fascination are also imagination. The Truth is very simple, but the human ego cannot take it so easily. The Truth states "there is only THIS", referring to the timeless moment as eternal Being. In other words, since THIS is all there is, who is it that reincarnates? Who is it that gets through a seeming journey?

Any aspects of "before" or "after" are just imagination. There is only THIS! Anything else is just movement created by the earth's rotation around the sun, creating the semblance of time and biological change, yet nothing is ever happening.

Fascination is the attractive force to the person seeking a better life, but not yet ready for the ultimate truth.

One time I was about to pass out and I even said to myself, "I am losing consciousness." So, I was aware that I was about to lose consciousness. And, on seeing this, that I am LIFE, I became conscious of Awareness. Awareness has always been here but it was not in my Consciousness. If consciousness and Awareness are different, will I still be conscious after death?

First, know that in truth, you are a BEING playing the human role. The BEING is pure Awareness, which is not a state but the aliveness that had never known a beginning and therefore is timeless. This is your true nature.

When the "Fall" of man occurred, known as the Big Bang, and the human form manifested, there also emerged the mind, which is thought. This is the birth of consciousness.

When you were ready to pass out, it was Awareness that saw clearly the losing of consciousness. Awareness can never be lost because it doesn't exist as "something." It JUST IS!

Through the birth of consciousness was also born the split known as duality. This was the birth of the human and also the birth of the ego idea.

Consciousness appears as the form and manifestation of the world. It is the world of mind. Mind, once created, also created the idea of time, as if there is a before and after. Therefore, Awareness is THIS, as you read these words. Awareness is timeless and always this moment. It is eternal because it doesn't know beginning or ending.

Mind, once created, became an integral part of Awareness and the two worked together. Being born human also meant being the BEING of pure Awareness…a human BEing.

We can lose consciousness, yet we cannot lose Awareness. Awareness has no existence because it is existence itself. Unfortunately the mind, being consciousness, cannot understand Awareness because it far above its scope of understanding.

When we awaken and see clearly that we are Awareness itself, known also as Presence, it is at this point that both Awareness and consciousness become one. We will be able to see clearly that the world is the creation of imagination and illusory.

When we, through the grace of awakening, start seeing our true nature as BEING (pure Awareness), it is then that we understand the mind's consciousness and its creation.

You mentioned how seeking the truth prevents us from seeing it. Is that why it takes so long to actually wake up to our true nature?

Yes! Initially, we live life like a robot in a very unconscious way and never question it. We just suffer and believe that Life is like this suffering. Then, we start questioning about God (which is love) and why this is so. We start hearing that LOVE is the only thing that works and go in search for it. We start seeking God, believing it is something we are going to attain or find, but it keeps eluding us by the very fact of seeking it.

How can you find your own BEING when you seek it somewhere else? BEING is God, Love, Truth, and we are that very Being. You are a human Being; a Being playing the role of human.

The human can't help seeking because it always feels a lack, a lack which is brought on by thinking it is a human person rather than BEING itself. Do you see the vicious circle that brings so much suffering?

CHAPTER TWENTY

There is No One to Forgive

I have just watched your satsang video on the Secret of Forgiveness, #30. You talked about when people hurt us, when they say things that upset us, it only hurts because we think we are a person and we identify with it. I'm also aware of your teachings about love and fear being the two basic emotions - all other emotions are products of those two basic emotions.

So I was thinking that when we have been offended or upset, it's the basic fear emotion that is playing out in us. I guess it's the fear of not being good enough, the fear of losing a job, etc. I find fear is very primitive, and deep down it always leads to the fear for survival. I think it's called the R complex part of the brain responsible for this.

So trying to forgive others essentially leads us back to forgiving ourselves (and vice versa) or the allowing of that fear or maybe the allowing of duality itself. It's unavoidable. It seems to be one and the same thing and proves how we are all connected in the oneness.

I think it's hard to do and involves taking that leap that you also refer to. It's almost like being told you can fly and standing at the edge of a cliff having never flown before, wondering if you can really do it, hahaha. A leap of faith :0)

I wonder which comes first the leap or the feeling, knowing that allows us to take the leap with confidence?

I remember as a kid the first time I went on a roller coaster, it took me all day to build up the courage to do it, and then after the first time I couldn't get enough it was so much fun.

My conclusion is this: before trying to forgive anyone, make sure you've forgiven yourself first.

It was a pleasure reading your sensitive and intelligent e-mail. You wrote… "My conclusion is this: before trying to forgive anyone, make sure you've forgiven yourself first."

There is no difference between the two. All is One. When you forgive another, you automatically forgive yourself. Feel it out, my friend. People ordinarily find it easier to forgive another than themselves, and so do it that way and it will come back being the same.

The *Course* says the following, and may the following guide you always:

"Nothing real can be threatened
Nothing unreal exists!"

What is real? It is that which never changes. Your body changes, your name can change, your job can change and your moods can change, but there's one thing that never ever changes. It is the ONE that sees these changes and that is changeless. The YOU that never changes is the ONE that is aware.

Thoughts change and we can be aware of thoughts. Awareness never changes. Awareness is LOVE itself because when unhampered by conditioned, fearful thoughts, Awareness is like an innocent child – free, happy and forgiving in a natural way.

I love dogs, kittens, puppies, because their love is constant, unless they are maltreated. You can know what is real in your feeling nature by asking this when you don't feel happy, ***"How would I rather feel right now rather than this stress?"***

Immediately your intuitive heart will respond, "I would rather feel whole!"

Listen to your heart always, because it is the essence of you. What is unreal changes, fluctuates, shifts and is unreliable and untrue. In truth, stress doesn't exist because it is NOT real. Therefore, when the conditioned ego makes you fearful, ashamed, and guilty or not feel good enough, learn to laugh at it and never take it seriously. This will be the beginning of seeing the Truth always and living it.

I want to thank you for your advice. What you suggested started working out soon! Very often, when I'm not aware enough, I start to fall back into this old pattern of ego control. How can I BE this BEING when the ego is so strong and drags me into every possible direction but the one that leads to love?

The ego is a conditioned concept. Therefore you have to be persistent in your seeing. Seeing is all that's necessary. The word "seeing" refers to letting our essence see the truth. We can know what is true in our heart by asking, ***"How would I prefer to feel instead of this?"***

This question will reveal the answer immediately by responding, "I'd rather feel whole!"

Because your BEING is Whole (complete with nothing missing).

Ego, on the other hand, is conditioned by man-made rules, conditions, unaware teachers in school, by adults who should have known better, by remarks that hurt us when young, by beliefs that were not real, by the way you see yourself in your mind (self-image), and so on.

Your thoughts will keep on repeating what you have been used to. You have to persist by seeing what is true, by asking your heart, "How do I prefer to feel instead of this?"

This way you will realize that your heart is your very BEING nature. Every time you lean towards your true nature, the easier it gets, until one day you'll be living from it most of the time.

I feel confused. You have said that there is no individual (separate person) and yet you say to forgive, to allow, to accept and to love. If there is no individual person then who is doing all this?

Thank you. Your question is a common one, until we start seeing the truth as it happens. The word "seeing" is not thinking, figuring out, concluding or intellectual activity.

Seeing is far superior to understanding intellectually. Seeing is what truly matters because it is the action of the Being, our true intuitive heart.

Please listen carefully and DO NOT try to figure this out. When the word acceptance is used, your intuitive heart knows that there's nothing to accept. Isn't that acceptance?

Here's an example. Suppose you told your son not to associate with children of a different race. He doesn't understand without being told why this is so.

He plays with those children anyway. In other words, he accepts them without the effort of accepting them. It is a natural way of BEING, isn't it?

The same way, when I say love, forgive, allow, surrender, let go and so on, all I am saying is emphasizing BEING. This is NOT a "doing" but simply BEING.

Someone asked me recently, "Burt you keep saying to allow. Who is it that allows if there is no controlling ego?"

You see, allowing means there is no one to allow and so allowing is a natural BEING with what is. Not only is there no effort in allowing but there is not even a thought associated with it. The word "allowing" is simply a reminder that there's nothing to do.

When a very depressed woman was ready to commit suicide and I asked her how depression felt, she said it felt like total helplessness. I asked her what helplessness was like when she "saw" it the way it really was. She was intelligent enough to "see" it like it was, and also "saw" that there was nothing she could do about it, absolutely nothing. That became allowing, accepting, forgiving and loving…it is BEING.

The moment she saw it clearly, she actually woke up, and she just gave her first talk to a group of people regarding this awakening to Being.

The reason there is confusion, frustration, mixed feelings, perplexity is because we try to figure things out, to think about them instead of allowing ourselves to SEE what is so very simple and obvious.

This is why Jesus admonished us to be like little children who are innocently allowing, forgiving and being who they are. Truth is always hiding in plain sight. The mind never sees the truth, but the innocent and uncomplicated always SEE it! This SEEING is known as spiritual intelligence.

When it is said that the ego has no choice, do people not have a choice to murder?

The ego is the conditioned part of the human that has forgotten its own Being. In other words, you are a human being; a Being playing the human role. When there is no awareness of this fact, then the ego lives from its unconscious drives, stories, conditioning and beliefs.

The ego cannot choose because ego acts through unconscious thoughts, emotions and drives. It reacts. Murder is not a direct choice of the ego. It acts through greed, hate, malice, guilt and fear, and so the body simply reacts. Even when murder is pre-meditated, it is still not a choice but a conditioned response from separation.

I will say to you, "You can't even choose to raise your arm."

The ego will feel challenged and raise its arm to prove me wrong. The arm raising wasn't a choice but a reaction of getting its own way. Do you see the point?

The ego is incapable of making a pure direct choice. This is hard to understand until we realize that our true nature is the Being playing the role of a human ego.

If there is only one ego, why do some steal and cheat and others do not?

There is only one ego and it functions from the belief in separation, filled with fear, doubt, suspicion, greed and selfishness. When someone acts from ego, they all act in a childish or immature way because the ego wants to get its own way, sometimes at all costs. When someone acts from ego, the action shows up in all humans the same way. They all act from that one ego.

To repeat, all characteristics of the ego are the same when someone is functioning from the ego.

The ones that are not greedy, fearful or selfish do not hurt or steal because they feel love. When someone loves you, at that very moment there is no ego.

Ego is that part in us that believes it is separate from Being (Christ-Self).

If BEING is all there is in Truth, then is Christ doing the murdering?

You are a human being; a Being playing the human role. Every human is really the essence of the Christ Self which is unconditional love. Now ask yourself, how can love hurt another willfully?

In order to understand the dynamics of your question, then see it this way. The BEING we are is love, safety, security, happiness, peace, comfort and inner Silence. This Being is the Christ-Self in us and is US. It gives us hints of its glory by expressing its essence of Light.

This is why if we ask, "How do I prefer to feel instead of feeling stressed?" immediately the intuitive heart or essence of you will answer, "I want to feel whole, complete, happy, fulfilled."

Why? In truth, you are the Christ-Self, meaning all these things of love. Now let's take a step further and understand what happens when we are depressed, frightened and act crazy. It happens this way...

You are a human being, a Being playing the human role. Even though you want love, security, safety and fulfillment, you still identify with the human-ego and so, when the Being gives you hints of security, you interpret it as a need for security because you identify with the human ego, limitation, a feeling of lack.

You don't see security as you are, but only as you wish to be, and security becomes the **need** for security. The need for security translates into insecurity. Got it?

It is the same with love. The Being showers you with love, but you, in turn, see it as a need for love because you think you are a small ego and therefore not good enough.

This need for love becomes a seeking of love, which is followed by getting easily hurt, feeling rejected, feeling lonely and even seeking others to love you. The Internet is filled with people seeking love because they cannot love themselves.

It is not Christ-Being which commits a murder, but the frustration, confusion, greed and fear that is usually followed with hate and revenge that commits the murder. All a misinterpretation of the great potential love we are. We twist it into its opposite because we cannot appreciate our greatness.

Our greatness is perfect love, but it is not an ego; it is the Oneness-Being we truly are. I hope that this is clear about choice, and the actions from either Being or ego.

You talk about Being as being everything, and that my true nature is Being and therefore, who I think I am doesn't exist but only as an image. Can you elaborate?

Being is the Oneness of life that appears in multiplicity, that is, as different humans. All desire, motivation, choice, love, safety, security, meaning and so on all come from Being.

Being is all there is, but it appears as if there is a human. This human is an appearance of Being. Being is our true Home. There is no happiness, safety nor security in the world of form unless there is this recognition that the Being is the only Truth.

The human is a self-image collected and accumulated from the past. It contains memories of all experiences and therefore identification with it is understandable.

When we seem to make choices, these choices are based on our past conditioned view of life, our so-called choices that happen so many times a day such as what to eat, clothes to put on, what tie to wear, what place to visit, where to go for fun and the choice in food.

All are based on our interpretation of our viewpoint of life. The choices we make in our relationships are often dictated by our past conditioned attractions. Our past dictates our life, ordinarily as an ego.

We are completely convinced that we are a person living a life, making the most of it, making decisions and choosing our life-partners and so on.

Little do we realize that even the choices we make are derived from how we see life, which is our viewpoint interpretation. However, everything that we believe we are deciding and choosing and seemingly controlling are all directed and orchestrated by Oneness. The script has been written. We are merely going through the motions as if we are in charge.

This life we seem to be living now has already happened, and our repetition is merely to "undo" the egoic-identity through forgiveness, also termed as letting-go, surrender, allowing, embracing, accepting and so on. We are to "re-learn" or "re-cognize" the BEING we are.

In our so-called life, we catch glimpses of the truth that help us look deeper. These glimpses help us to see how Oneness is "doing" everything. Our every desire is a secret longing to go Home – to Being! Everything happens through Being (Oneness, God, Love, Allness).

We get glimpses of our true nature, which is Being recognizing itself. After all, the nature of Awareness is Self-recognizing.

A few years ago I "saw" my life pass before me and witnessed that all the major events and aspects of life were not chosen by "me" at all. They happened.

Nothing is ultimately ever chosen. The whole dream of choice and motivation seems to exist only in our initial intellectual understanding based on separation in time and space.

We had believed that there was something in time that moved forward with intention from a place called duality to a place called oneness. We were not "ready" to see yet that a human being is BEING playing the human role. There has never been anything but Being, and this is the eternal nothing and everything.

Initially, we wanted to believe we were controlling Being by our spiritual fascination. We moved from playing to seeing. Seeing, and not intellectual comprehension, understanding or practice that did it but, the readiness to finally see what is.

Being is not going anywhere. Being was never born and knows no death. Being is not attained nor understood. Being has never been anywhere but everywhere. There was no time or space, but only the appearance of them, until we looked deeper and saw deeper. There is nothing but THIS! This is IT! All that is necessary is to SEE it!

CHAPTER TWENTY ONE

I'M LOOKING BUT I CAN'T SEE IT

How do we get ready to see?

There is nothing we can do about readiness, since the human-ego has no power to choose or do. However, if these words strike home then readiness is happening. It is all in the SEEING and not understanding intellectually. Seeing is our intuitive heart, which is directly connected with Being (Oneness).

The material in *A Course in Miracles,* when grasped intuitively, can bring recognition. The *Course* states:

Nothing real can be threatened.
Nothing unreal exists.
Herein lies the peace of God.

What if you actually heard those words? What if those very words shook you to the core? Did you know that those few words say it all?

The word "you" is used to point to Being. The word you refer to All That IS! There is no specific singular you, but Being looking from billions of viewpoints, and yet there is Nothing and Everything at once.

When I hear the words regarding Being, I get scared. The human is still very real to me and I don't want to treat it as if it doesn't exist. Can you talk about balance?

You are a human being; a Being playing the human role. Therefore the human role is important, with all its thoughts, emotions and various feelings. It is the human in you that creates the fear. In the

Being there is no fear, therefore there is also love and respect for the human appearance. It is all part of the play.

The human is important and needs to be integrated into its Oneness. If you deny any part of the human then you also deny the truth. It is through the human that we wake up. It is through darkness that we grope for the Light.

The Being is acceptance, love, completion, surrender, letting-go, forgiveness... BE-ing is everything. The true devotee of Truth accepts everything AS IS! There is nothing to fear since nothing REAL can be threatened, and nothing unreal can exist!

Although the human is an appearance of Being, it is a but a role we must play. It is in the playing, laughter and enjoyment that the Being is celebrated. When you know BEING, then the human is not disregarded but becomes the catalyst for allowing, enjoying and celebrating.

Did you know that all longing in the human is for Home, which is Being? Did you know that all of the human's seeking is for the Being? Did you know that the human cannot enjoy laughter, joy, happiness or peace until it is expressing Being?

The human and all of its judgments, fears, problems, emotional suffering is nothing more than a need for the Being! Why not allow the human to be what it is in full acceptance as the smooth way to go Home to Being?

I know that you have discussed this law of mind called "The Law of Attraction," but I am still not clear why there's so much fuss about this new law when it is obvious?

The Law of Attraction is NOT a new law but as old as humans. This law came into Being the moment the Big Bang started creation.

This law says "You become that which you imagine to be." What you believe manifests.

This law is based on imagination. Also, the world that we experience as real is all imagination. Look at any human being and you will see, in an obvious way, the Law of Attraction at work. How?

As I was walking yesterday going to the bank, there was a young man sitting in the street begging for money. Isn't it obvious how he sees himself and the world he experiences? That's the Law of Attraction. We attract and manifest that which we carry in our focus.

What we fear, hate or love manifests accordingly. When the movie *The Secret* was produced, many people believed it was really a secret that was never known.

Admittedly, the movie was genius despite its hype. It made it seem that The Law of Attraction is something new that was hidden from the public. In truth all great men, including basic psychology, have told us that we become what we believe. This movie carried the message effectively, but it didn't tell you the whole truth.

The real secret is the BEING, but if it was made into a movie then nobody would watch it. No human wants the truth since the human is a seeker for more and more.

The Truth is Being, which means there is no such thing as you, but only as Oneness appearing as you. No human wants to lose their personal identity. What they don't realize is that there never was or could ever be a personal identity.

We hear often people saying, "My life is difficult," or "Why is this happening to my life?" The Truth is not welcome here because it is this which is truth. There is no such thing as "my" life and there never was. There is only LIFE!

Even if we say there is only now, then the mind will refer to now as "now and then." If the word "this moment" is used, then the mind would ask, "What about the next moment?"

The mind is always thinking in linear time and it can't be helped. This is why listening to our intuitive heart beyond mind is the key. There is only THIS! It is aliveness. THIS is what we can refer to as Aliveness. Aliveness is Beingness. It is directly this that lives forever without beginning or end. All there is, is what is arising!

The dream refers to THIS as what is happening to me. This is the hypnotic dream that is the basic belief of most people, until they awaken to the truth that never changed.

The movie *The Secret* makes it seem that we can have anything we want. As far as material acquisition is concerned, it is true if we want it badly enough. However, there's another aspect we cannot have through imagination and that is security, safety, love, fullness, peace and realization of truth.

The human tries to get these things by accumulating wealth and power, but the price is devastating. Many extremely wealthy people die in desperation because they still fear death, the end of their dream, and so where was security or safety?

When we wake up to the truth of our Being, then we have security, peace, safety, love and fullness because BEING is these very things. The human is always chasing after the Being but doesn't know it. Since there is no awareness of this, it translates into the accumulation of material goodies. The unaware mind says, "If I can have wealth and power, then I can have what I want."

Here's the million dollar question: "What is it you really want through wealth and power?"

Isn't it the reinforcement of the me, so that it can feel free and happy and do what it wants? But the sad joke is this; there is no me and there never was. You are a human being; a Being playing the human role.

There is something that I do not understand. Here is my question. Since the human is basically fear and the Being is love, how are they basically One Whole?

The human is motivated by the survival instinct and the need to maintain its own illusory duality. This need is basic; therefore the attachment to the me-identity. The me, while feeling separate from the Being, develops a great need for love, which is also the Being's true influence of Wholeness; thus, there seems to be a split between human and Being.

This split is often referred to in the *Course* as split-mind. It is illusory, and so any efforts for the human to gain control of love merely boomerang into fear. This fear, which is fear of intimacy, fear of rejection, fear of feeling unloved and unwanted, fear of not bonding or being good enough and so on, is simply the belief that we are separate from our true nature, which is the Being. In this case, we come to know something very simple. All fear is really a frustration of love.

Now when we resist fear, like thinking "I shouldn't be afraid" or "this is wrong" or "I am missing something" and so on, we are also creating a separation from our true nature, the Being.

What if we accepted the fear as a natural longing for what we are? What if we didn't resist the fear at all and allowed it as part of our need for love and therefore a hunger for wholeness?

Once you bring fear into your welcoming arms as something to "learn," then fear and love bond and Wholeness feeling results.

Until we recognize who we really are, our life is largely driven by the things we fear. When we recognize fear as an unconscious need for wholeness, then we see that fear is a frustration of love and no longer something "bad," but rather, something we need to learn from.

The basic fear of the human is loss of self because there is the belief that one is an ego called me. The fear of losing yourself is what perpetuates and sustains the ego drive for improving, gaining, accomplishing, attaining, overcoming, resisting and need for power. In this need is also created the idea of beginning and ending, and holding on to what we believe we might lose.

Fearing weakness, we strive for control. Fearing intimacy, we strive to be aloof. Fearing subservience, we strive to be dominant. If we fear being ordinary, then we try to be special.

The things that the human fears are endless, because if one fear is overcome, we put another one in its place. For example, "What if I awaken and then I couldn't relate to people anymore?"

"What if through realizing my true nature I lose connection with the human side of me?"

Human fears are endless, and even when we come close to rising above them, then another fear takes its place. This is the domain of the illusory ego.

If the story that engenders the fear is dropped, all that we are left with is a physical sensation that is raw and alive. Now, seeing the truth that fear was just a story of the mind, we take our place in existence without bondage and see everything as it actually is. This freedom is the liberating of our true nature.

If we cease labeling fear as bad and mine, and simply allow it as energy in a certain form, it can then begin to have its own flavor that will take us deeper into glorious Presence. It is here that both duality and Oneness are seen as One.

I am studying* A Course in Miracles *and it states that unconscious guilt is imbedded in our unconscious and it is this that gives us the feeling we are unworthy and undeserving. Can you explain?

The unconscious refers to a memory that we are not conscious of at all. First of all, do not be concerned about something you cannot handle in the moment, such as unconscious memory. Rather, see that only THIS truly matters. Forget about unconscious stuff that is beyond your seeing.

Suffice it to say that guilt is a feeling of having done something wrong even though you might not know what that is. When guilt persists like a pebble in your shoe when you walk, there comes a point where you desperately want to get rid of it. This need to get rid of this feeling becomes often a projection towards another.

Take the case of Mary, who was abused by her father as a young girl. She grew up distrusting men. When she met a man who she felt was sincere and truly caring for her, she would find excuses not to love and eventually leave him. These excuses could be anything that this man said or did that triggered Mary's self-sabotage to blame the innocent party as a form of "getting rid of this guilt."

Guilt always projects its nagging feeling and often finds excuses to sabotage what it wants most.

When we expend energy in feeling guilty and attempting to assuage that illusory sense, we negate the possibility of liberation. We get stuck from moving towards Being.

The reason guilt is so tenacious is because there is both a fascination and indulgence built into the drama of sin and karma. It is often witnessed that the guilt takes off a dramatic turn of hysteria or even violence.

When there is a love of the Being that we are, there is also the experiencing of Presence. In Presence there is no becoming, no attachment to a goal and no need to overcome the guilt. This Presence I refer to as the Holy Spirit. It is the Wholeness as Spirit essence.

We start seeing, through this love, that there is no longer a need to achieve any standard of behavior to become worthy. This love for the Holy Spirit and worthiness become One Thing.

In Presence there is no debt to pay because there is no history. In any situation, either there is a feeling of separation or there is Presence. In Presence, the self (me) is no more and there is simply that which Is!

In this simplicity of seeing, all concepts of good or bad, original sin, karma or debts of any kind are now seen as the products of an unawakened mind that is locked into time.

I am still not clear what Presence is. Can you explain in simple terms?

There are no words that can explain what Presence is any more than I can explain what the color red looks like to a blind man. Words are symbols and pointers. But the reason teachers talk to a group, and books are written by awakened beings, is because when one is ready, it is their intuitive heart that resonates and not the conditioned intellect.

Please know that intellectual understanding is not enough, because it lacks direct knowing that only the readiness of the heart can know. Once you feel that reading this book and its words become an exciting adventure to you, then you are definitely resonating with it. It is this resonance that takes you one step further into intuitive knowing.

Whenever I am asked to explain what Presence is, I say, "Holy Spirit," with whom I talk daily and receive inspired messages. Visualize, for the sake of replying to your question, that there's a witness as if he/she is overlooking your every thought, emotion and movement, without judgment but with total, compassionate love.

In Presence there is the clear seeing that you have never chosen or done anything, but that Life lives through you, acting as "you." You are a Being playing the human role.

In this acceptance of my divine helplessness, I enjoy the freedom of never having a past or future I could call my own.

When people ask you, "Who directs this Life?" you might not have to answer, or care to. While in the arms of the Beloved, nothing matters. I can live as though I choose, and rejoice in the letting go.

A lot of emphasis has been placed on the self-image. Is it really that important to know about?

The famous Roberto Assagioli, the Founder of Psycho-Synthesis, wrote, "Ninety-five percent of our energy is spent protecting, defending and maintaining our self-image and its all imagination."

The self-image is a creation of our mind, based on the way we have been brought up to believe we are. Although the self-image is unconscious, it affects every part of our life.

When a client comes to see me, I get an immediate glimpse of their self-image by the way they walk, talk, express and how their eyes move during talking. This image is buried deep in their unconscious.

One time during a workshop, I asked the people to draw how they see themselves, their image of themselves. Most had great difficulty. In fact, most didn't even know they had a self-image.

When we react to how people treat us, it presents a perfect example of our self-image and how we protect it. What do you feel causes people to get offended, hurt or threatened? Isn't it because there was a jolt to their self-image?

The self-image is the ego part of us and it is the reason we carry guilt, shame, fear and a hundred other uncomfortable feelings. They all have to do with the self-image. Remember the man who just wanted a successful business, whose father called him a klutz as a child?

Since he didn't know about this picture of himself, he started looking deeper into his true nature as Being playing the human role. Years later he developed a successful business.

The Law of Attraction is the law of mind, and it is a powerful law because it brings to you what you focus on. You may be induced to start picturing success as *The Secret* suggested, but unless you see how you actually see yourself, and also what you keep thinking about yourself, then you draw to you what you have been focusing on.

Why is it that no matter what we tell ourselves, such as "I want success or abundance," it doesn't happen most of the time?

There are two reasons for that. First, it is what your subconscious mind believes that manifests. Secondly, what you tell yourself you want is often a cover-up for what you truly want.

If you have often felt that you are not good enough (unworthy), then picturing yourself very wealthy would "cover-up" your self-image of failure.

If you ever dreamed of owning millions of dollars, then this did not mean that that was what you really wanted. It meant that you could "play" being important or successful with so much money. What you really wanted was a better ego than you had.

When people go for power, wealth and material gain it is because there is a need to cover up deep feelings of personal failure. This is the reason why crime bosses insist on having power and being respected, because deep inside they have a very poor picture of themselves.

There is only one way to have a good self-image and that is when you see yourself as Wholeness rather than a personal self. You see that there is no personal self, but One-Self. Life itself! It is the only key to true love, peace, security, safety and fullness of Being.

Can one feel fulfilled without spiritual awakening?

You can answer that question yourself by asking, "Can I be fulfilled as a human being, when this human being doesn't know who he is yet?"

Everybody in the world for whom awakening hasn't happened feels alienated. Whether there is a war going on, or whether you live in a beautiful penthouse in New York, all the time there is a sense of separation, the feeling that something is missing.

After awakening, that apparent life story still goes on as before, but the identification with it is totally lost. You simply discover that you are still a human being, but BEING playing the human role.

What is it that we really want? What is the human yearning for? You say "Being," but Being to me is meaningless and nothingness. Please help me understand?

Strange how the human mind makes something simple so complicated. Of course, there is a great mystery in life, and one that our puny minds can't even begin to scratch.

However, what we all want is very basic, and that is the expression of life itself, known as fullness or wholeness. The word "Being" truly implies nothingness from which everything emerged. All of life as we know it emerged from Nothingness.

Can we understand this nothingness? Can we understand what non-duality is, which the nature of this nothingness is? Of course, not!

However, we can recognize our true nature as this nothingness (Being) and so we can rise above our daily disturbed mind, which is ever-so-filled with the personal self that it can't find rest anywhere.

By seeing that our daily mind is time-bound in a universe that is beyond time and space, we can release the truth that we are far more than just an individual personal self. This is not difficult at all because, after all, it is our true nature.

It happens by simply being (BE-ing), also known as allowing, accepting, loving, forgiving and letting-go of all that which is not real.

What is true right now? Isn't it right now? Isn't it this moment without a next moment, since THIS moment is forever? Is there really a past or is it just history that our mind enjoys reveling into? Is there a tomorrow or is it just another misconception because THIS moment has no exit?

When you recognize this simple truth, which is hiding in plain sight, then you'll begin to live with a whole new energy! You'll start feeling and living alive to the point where THIS IS ALL THERE IS!

It might not be easy at first because the individual personal mind will come up with a thousand questions. However, remaining alert HERE-NOW, knowing it is all you can ever know or be, you relax. With this recognition, the mystery starts unfolding on its own good time as we are ready for it.

Awakening is simply seeing the obvious and then allowing it fully. It is this allowing itself which brings our inner security and inner safety and love to its full expression. How?

LOVE and SECURITY are non-existent in the mind; they only express fully in nothingness known as absence of self.

What do we all want and yearn for? Isn't it obvious? It is for our true nature of nothingness, which is also experienced as peace, love, security, safety, happiness and above all – aliveness! After all, nothingness is everything, just like everything is nothingness!

CHAPTER TWENTY TWO

The Good Life

All my life I thought that true living is living the good life. What is a good life anyway?

Funny you should ask that question. For many years I used to feel bad for telling untruths or exaggerating, which is typical of my enneagram #7.

It was after my awakening in the year 2000 that I saw clearly that living the true life has nothing to do with being good but simply seeing Oneness and that was it.

After all, Oneness does everything through us and acts as us. How I behave has nothing to do with the truth. This was also made clear in *A Course in Miracles*. If I see myself as the Oneness acting through me, then what else do I need?

In my life I have seen many so-called good people harboring resentments and unloving thoughts. When I witnessed on television the people who thought they were good people flying an airplane into the World Trade Center, I saw what good people can do.

During the war, the Nazis believed God was on their side. When I explored the thinking and believing of these good people who killed so many Americans in the World Trade Center massacre, I realized fully that these people were doing the right good thing (what they believed) and as a result, they would go to heaven for killing Americans.

Being good has nothing to do with being TRUE! Many religious people believe they are good people by going to church on Sundays and doing good, while harboring thoughts and beliefs in separation. Being good has nothing to do with LOVE.

The good life is a conditioned idea how things should be. It has nothing to do with LOVE, which is Truth and non-separation.

Being good is a façade, a veneer, and the belief that by being good, we are being spiritual. Our true nature has nothing to do with how to behave but only to FEEL LOVE and JOY in the heart. Once you feel joy and love, your actions express that despite innocent mischief or seeming outrageous behavior.

I remember a time when Rajneesh (now known as Osho) was regarded as a scoundrel and the good people in Oregon, where he had his Rajneeshpuram town, tried to kill him (and finally succeeded by poisoning him).

One time, I was walking around town in Oregon, close to Rajneeshpuram. I heard people say that Osho was a devil and should be annihilated.

When I sat with Osho in his small room I knew I was sitting with a truly great consciousness. It is true that his words and actions were often outrageous, but his Beingness was truly holy.

Now I am confused. Doesn't being awakened also follow being and doing good?

The whole of our appearance as a human being is merely a reflection of a longing to find that love which is totally beyond the concept of good and bad, right and wrong. The idea of goodness and badness is just a reflection of the real nature of things. The real nature of Oneness is that it is Unconditional Love. It is totally unassailable love without any sense of anything else. Our ideas of good and bad are simply a very tepid reflection of that.

What about teaching children to be good? Isn't that necessary?

Have you ever seen children growing up healthily when they were controlled in trying to be good? They ended up frustrated, unhappy, guilty and unable to be fully themselves.

The best way to bring up children is to love them unconditionally and then let them bring themselves up as they learned, at their own speed. All the guidance they needed was not how to behave, but to care and love. Once they had their freedom, then LOVE took over and led them where they were meant to be.

You are Being, playing the human role
No past – no future – only THIS!!

I was listening to one of your videos on YouTube when you emphasized that there is only this Moment. It stuck with me. Later, I entered a food store and there was that feeling that there was only this. It was a very relaxing soothing feeling. Can you comment?

These are moments of glimpsing the truth. By reading this book, which repeats over and over that you are a BEING, playing the role of human, something starts percolating in you in which your intuitive heart starts remembering its true nature. This remembering, however short-lived, is the glimpse of an awakening heart.

When there is only this, which is this moment without a next moment, then there is a sweetness that arises. "There is only this!"

Usually our mind makes it into something else and gets in the way of SEEING that there is only THIS! This is divine; this is Oneness; this is SEEING without the projected self. It is a fragrance of freedom, sweetness (BEING).

It occurred to me that searching for truth is like making love in an attempt to find pure love – which becomes a denying of pure love!

Searching for truth is denying it. It is like searching for the Oneness when all there is, is Oneness anyway. It blocks us from seeing the obvious. Oneness is ever hiding in plain sight.

When there is no "me," there is clear seeing. Everything is seen as it is. The me is a seeker and always looking for some answer, some justification that blocks the very seeing of the obvious. When the me is absent--that is, there is no one--everything is seen as floating in and is accepted just as it is, without judgment. It is accepted by no one since such acceptance is automatic, without anyone doing the accepting. There is no sense of there being an individual who things float into.

With no one being there to judge, everything flows and arises in love. Everything is love. There is no question of anything needing to change or anything needing to be different or better. It just IS what it is!

In one of your old videos you talked about the Beloved. Is the full acceptance of what-is, as it is, seeing the Beloved because nothing happens by chance?

Yes, since love is all there is and it is always Oneness acting. It is the Beloved One acting through you. In BEING the human role playing, there is also no me interfering or even making a choice.

There is a knowing, beyond question, that all decisions are being conducted by the BEING you already are. You are BEING playing the human role. It is resting in that whatever is happening is what needs to happen. You don't interfere because you see there is no me to interfere anyway.

Awakening is seeing of the one that seeks. And, in that seeing, there is also a cessation of the seeker, knowing because you know it doesn't work.

CHAPTER TWENTY THREE

WHAT HAPPENS TO THE "ME"?

What is unconditional love? Is it the acceptance of all that we think, feel, say, do and behave? Is it THIS as it actually IS?

It is great to get such an incredibly wonderful question.

This is really what unconditional love is. Through total self-acceptance, which is true compassion, what happens is that the me takes a back seat because it is also accepted by no one. When acceptance happens, there is also no one accepting, and that, my friend, is true acceptance. Acceptance is not something we do but it is a SEEING that there is no choice. It comes out of nothing.

You see, all the time there is someone there deciding, figuring out, thinking this and that, weighing, judging and questioning, and it is all wasted effort because the me is just a conditioned idea of mind. It is this activity that blocks us from true love. True love is the love that arises from unconditioned seeing and has nothing to do with anyone.

Is awakening simply clear seeing of what is, as unconditional love? If so, where does forgiveness come in?

Forgiveness seems to have many levels of understanding. Initially, people believe that forgiveness is the conventional way of doing it, like saying, "I forgive you!"

With increased seeing of unconditional love, that everything happens as it should and there are no mistakes, then forgiveness is seen as – there is nothing to forgive because nothing actually happened other than what is!

I am still not clear of how we drop the me. Please, can you make it clearer, as I feel quite caught in this idea?

The wonderful thing about the me idea is that we can start seeing that all sense of separation, all fear, all self-destructing behavior and all wars, conflicts, etc., have stemmed from the belief that there is a separate individual called me.

Once you glimpse this fact, even minutely, then you are ready to rise above it. Do you know how? By NOT dropping this belief at all!

Do you know why? Who is going to do it? So what is one to do, asks the me. Nothing, absolutely nothing, because there is only THIS! In the seeing of this, is also seeing that this moment is all there is. How can it be otherwise? Anything else is just mind gobbledygook!

Again, once seeing this fact, the dropping of the me falls away without any attempt to do so. You see, the me only exists in time, such as who you think you are (past) and what this me is going to do next (future).

When you see that there's only THIS, and it is neither good nor bad, neither right nor wrong, but just this happening, it had to happen. Why? Simply because it is happening! Then this very SEEING is the dropping of the me.

When you e-mailed me the reply to my question about dropping the "me," there was a sudden acceptance of the me being there, and seeing clearly how it was imposing itself on the original Oneness of Being. There was suddenly the feeling that I have been "playing this me all my life," such as seeking truth, wanting personal enlightenment, reaching some goals for success, making lots of money, getting somewhere and so on; t'was all about me. When I saw how, for so many years, I sought to change it all and immersed myself even deeper into this me idea, I also saw how difficult it was to allow it to be there without any sense that it could be different…

Yes, this seeing is the clarity of awakening. As a human, we are helpless to do anything, and it often takes us a whole lifetime to see something so obvious and simple.

When we get to know unconditional love, something else starts happening, which is that everything is okay as it is and there's nothing we can do, and no one that can remove the ego, to make things better or even to awaken.

In this seeing, there is a sudden feeling of relaxation, of BEING (to-be). It is here that we start to wake up to the fact that I AM BEING, playing the human role and everything is okay as it is! This is love manifesting. It is the return to innocence where the ideas of wrong, should, etc., fall away.

I was wondering if what we call me or ego is the same like daily mind?

They are different identities which we believe are who we are. There is the belief that the mind is a thing that actually exists. In truth, the individual mind is a mass of thoughts, and Bhagavan Ramana Maharshi made that clear.

Initially, the personal human tries to control the mind and get rid of painful thoughts, which merely exacerbates the situation. There is no one who can do such a thing because the removal of the personal individual mind is the same, like the me wanting to overcome itself.

There is only acceptance where no one does any accepting. Get the obvious point? It is all about SEEING, which is the enhancement of the BEING (the self-recognizing Awareness).

From that SEEING, there is the activation of self-organizational point of the Awareness taking care of the rest.

I have read that all negative feelings are fear-based. The* Course *says that all emotions are divided into two emotions, namely, love or fear. Can you explain further?

The *Course* says emphatically:

Nothing real can be threatened
Nothing unreal exists.
Herein lies the peace of God.

So very simple and direct, yet the mind finds it hard to accept. The reason the conditioned mind finds it hard to accept is because the egoic mind is all fear. Fear is self-perpetuating. It feeds on itself unendingly.

Even when we crave love so desperately, there is still doubt that we deserve it, it is too good to be true, or we resist it outright. This is all fear, including the doubt itself.

Here's the good news, if there is the willingness to hear it. Nothing unreal exists and fear is unreal. So now the question is, "Why do we have fear if it is so unreal?"

We were humanly born with the instinct of survival in order for the human to protect itself against the elements and survive. This instinct brought with it the fear of not surviving, and thus the fear of human death became an unconscious obsession.

This unconscious fear brought with it psychological fear, which is the culprit of modern stress, bringing with it depression, guilt, anger, anxiety and a hundred other fears.

Waking up to our true nature, which is Being, liberates us from fear. That's the plus of awakening. Also, nothing real can be threatened, and so we do not lose what we have discovered, which is LOVE. Love is the very nature of Being, and not an action or behavioral expression.

You are a human being; Being playing the human role, and therefore Oneness is the Truth that never changes. When we emphasize the human and forget the BEING, then we separate the two, and it is this very separation which brings suffering – deep-seated fear!

The best way to deal with fear is doing nothing but simply remaining in your BEING nature. Be-ing means "TO BE" with whatever is without even the need to alter it, get rid of it or control it in any way. This way you bring BE-ING into the fear, and the two enmesh and become ONE. Love is so all-encompassing that it can absorb any fear no matter how horrendous. In fact, fear, when fully understood, is the frustration of love. Allowing BEING (which is love) melts fear automatically and restores Oneness.

The words "allowing Being" are redundant because Be-ing means allowing, accepting, loving, surrendering, forgiving, letting-go. All are the expression of Being.

Since fear is instigated by the sense of separation (human and Being), then it merely reinforces the erroneous belief in the me that we have taken for granted. The greatest fear of the me is losing the me identity. The good news is that there never was a me to lose, since nothing unreal exists.

When fear is not met with BEING, then it perpetuates itself to the point of breakdown. Fear never stands still; it gains momentum because it wants something to be done, some control, resistance, and so it keeps adding to itself.

When the fear is met with BEING, just being and doing absolutely nothing, not even thinking about it or wishing it wasn't there, this nothingness, which is love, absorbs the fear.

The *Course* tells us, "You need do nothing."

The mind, which is constantly controlling, finds it immensely hard to do nothing. That's when we separate the men from the boys.

How does the daily mind work?

The daily mind is just a collection of thoughts. Thoughts are impressions, like clouds crossing the vast sky. They are unconscious pictures and create our so-called reality! It is all imagination. The world we experience is all the daily mind.

The daily mind, which we know as our personal mind, divides everything into two, such as duality. The mind is the divider. Take time-consciousness and division and there is no mind but enlightenment. And here's the good news. The mind becomes our servant, not our controller.

I can see that in Being there is no attainment nor a process, but does having had glimpses or experiences create an environment where you can easily reunite?

Yes, definitely! Even reading this book with an open heart and mind can actually activate your intuitive heart to have glimpses of the REAL.

Just as fear is darkness, so is love light. There is no such thing as darkness but simply dimmed light. Allowing the dimmed light as simply dimmed light will bring greater light. This allowing for a greater seeing is called "a glimpse."

I was reading Ramana Maharshi's teaching where he said that there is only the Self. Was he referring to Being by the word Self?

Yes. There is only Oneness. Oneness can be called Being, Self, Love, God, Source or Life, if you prefer. As we delve deeper and deeper into the Being we'll find ourselves seeing it everywhere and in everything.

I have found that the word LOVE is appropriate, as it is more of a natural expression. You will see it in a puppy's affection and eyes, you will see it in the kitten and in a child's eyes and laughter. This love is pure and innocent, which again makes us understand the Being.

When awakening to our true nature arises, we'll start seeing a whole new world. Love overruns and overturns this world and embraces it. It makes a nonsense of this world. The reality of love makes nonsense of the way we think the world is.

Just as the world teaches us to strive, to be hard-workers and to be doing all the time, love teaches us to relax and enjoy. In this love, we see there is nowhere to go. There has never been anywhere to go. It teaches us that what we looked for and struggled and searched was always here…our very Being.

There is only the One, which is the Source, the nothingness that appears as everything. You'll never feel alone because this Source is also Presence that never leaves you. This Presence, known as I AM, is forever acting through you.

No matter what I do, I can't get rid of negative thinking. It keeps coming back and it is relentless. What can I do?

Negative thinking repeats because, in a way, it is a comfort. The comfort is this – this is me. The greatest fear is the Truth of Being, which is Oneness.

The fact that you are BEING playing the human role is very scary to most people, even horrifying when the recognition smacks us in the face saying, "There is no personal identity."

And so, since this fear is mostly unconscious initially, we find comfort and protection in thinking negatively because, no matter how annoying and debilitating it is, it gives us the feeling that I am me.

The moment you start realizing there is no me, the negative thinking simply stops without any effort. It is this me that thinks negatively to keep the illusion of a separate personal self. It is this illusion that creates intense suffering and fear of death.

There is only one liberation from negative thinking, and that is SEEING your true nature as Oneness. Are you willing to do that?

Seeing your Oneness is not difficult, but it does require courage to face the Truth. If you can see right now how negativity keeps you locked into your personal self, then it is already a good start. Your next move is this: not to stop negative thinking (which is not possible), but to see that there is no me to indulge in it.

The reason I keep yearning for freedom is to be free from this feeling of personal responsibility. It feels like I carry a heavy load on my back.

What you said is a very common feeling. The reason it seldom happens is because your drive for truth is still the personal need. Truth means you are BEING playing the human role.

As long as you see yourself as a personal me, how can it happen? How can you be free, when you are still hanging on to that which is the burden itself?

It seems that living from the One Being and discarding the personal self is a tall order and one that most people are incapable of. Am I correct in this?

First of all, it is not a tall order because it is the Truth already happening. It is not something you are going to attain. You are already BEING playing the human role. Secondly, believing it as a tall order is the big block to seeing it.

The aspect of living from BEING, because you are simply role-playing, is not difficult at all. It is already happening. So to repeat, why are you unwilling to see it?

Yes, it is scary and our conditioning will create all kinds of excuses and fears not to SEE it, so it is a matter of allowing it and NOT doing anything.

There is no personal self to do anything except in our conditioned self-image. Once you see the fear, you have taken your first big step. The second step is to start forgiving it (with compassion).

You keep mentioning the word Seeing – can you please make it clear what that means?

As a human being, there are many ways in which we expand our awareness of Being. We have basic intellectual understanding, which results from reading and study. Then we have the open heart that goes deeper. Third, we have the unmistakable intuition that comes from opening the heart. Finally, from the open intuitive heart we have the clarity of seeing.

Seeing is far superior to the intellect, to reason, to deduction, etc., for it is actually intelligence inherent in our innocence that sees what is (prior to conditioning).

This is why children see things that we miss altogether. However, the children see the truth, but they can't put it in words and have no means of expressing it. This is why children start acting up against parents, not because they are bad, but because they see the absurd behavior of quarreling, conflicts, crazy behavior of adults and their gossip and meaningless chatter about meaningless things.

Seeing is the only "thing" necessary for awakening. That is, seeing what is! For example, how often do you get caught in a negative thought and start feeling unhappy or miserable? Seeing what is, is very simple.

A thought is seen as a thought and that's it. It is like looking at the sky and seeing the clouds. Then a cloud covers up the sun and you feel bad for having the sun covered and not getting your warmth or tan. Yet what has actually happened?

Seeing implies an open, innocent heart that is allowing itself to see what is, as it actually IS!

You sit still and allow yourself to see who you are at this very moment. It gets scary initially when you see that you are nothing. However, let's assume you still sincerely want to see what is. What happens?

You will see what is, which is watching what is, as it is. Get it? Therefore, you see that SEEING is pure Awareness recognizing itself.

It is through sincere and dedicated SEEING that we realize the truth eventually.

CHAPTER TWENTY FOUR

PEACE OF MIND DOES NOT EXIST

In one of the videos you talked about the method of CRIF and it has helped me, but I often get mixed up about how to do it when I am caught in emotional pain. Can you explain it further?

The most important thing to understand is that it is NOT a method to do, but a SEEING. Seeing is all that's necessary for us to live the true life.

Seeing means feeling/knowing/listening without effort because the heart is open. So when you look at anything with an open heart, that is, without trying to figure it out, without even thinking about it but actually SEEING IT AS IT IS, then a whole new way of comprehension arises that goes straight to the heart.

The truth is this moment, simply because this moment is all there is. This moment is Oneness. Many people have heard this statement that THIS MOMENT IS ALL THERE IS, but not many have seen it, as it actually is.

Suppose you become very still right now and listen to the following: THIS moment is all you can have or be for there is nothing else. This moment is beyond time because there is no past. The past is history. There is no future. The future is not yet and hasn't happened yet. Therefore we are always HERE forever.

Also, there is no EXIT to now. Wherever you are and whatever you are doing or not doing, IT IS ALWAYS THIS MOMENT! When the past happened, it wasn't the past, it was this moment! All happening happens now. Nothing can happen outside of now because it is impossible. This is the Truth of BEING

If you have a glimpse of this MOMENT and have seen the eternal in it, which means no exit, then you have all the answers to life. Why does it have all the answers?

Feel it now, that you may SEE it! THIS MOMENT means that it is your true nature. When you say, "I am being now," you have lost it. You cannot be this moment; you cannot attain this moment; you cannot hold on to this moment. Why?

LISTEN CAREFULLY. There is no you but this moment itself. Wherever you go, there you are! Therefore, to repeat, there is no you, but only THIS MOMENT, known as Oneness.

What seems to be you is only the past conditioning. The real YOU is this MOMENT! Do you get it now? If you do, then you have SEEN it in your intuitive heart.

THIS IS WHO YOU ARE! It seems that is a separate you, but it is a mirage. YOU ARE THIS MOMENT playing the role of human.

Now, having grasped the above with your open intuitive heart, we can start understanding CRIF. CRIF stands for...

CHOICE

RESPONSIBILITY

IMAGINATION

FORGIVENESS

When you use this CRIF at the moment of emotional pain, then this is how it is applied with the understanding you have opened from THIS MOMENT!

Emotional pain happens in the moment. At the moment you feel it. Do you have a choice in getting rid of it right away? Do you have a choice in pretending it is not there?

No, there is no choice because you are caught in it. This also means that although it is happening in the moment, it happened because it recalled some past identification. There's nothing you can do, right? Allow yourself to see you have no choice but to allow it.

This allowing is called responsibility. Response-ability means to respond to the moment, as it is. Again, allowing it to be, as it is, because there is no choice in the moment, is responsibility in the moment.

You know very well that if you resist it by wishing it wasn't there, it will get worse. If you tried to do something about it or feel guilty for having it, then you are still resisting. So, the key is to do nothing whatever.

The third item is imagination. Imagination simply means mind. All thoughts and emotions are impressions; mental pictures, no matter how subtle. All thoughts and emotions are imagination. They cannot be real unless we make them feel real, but then, that's how we live in illusion.

So, at this point, you SEE that whatever is in this MOMENT as a thought is just imagination. How else can it be? Just look at it. Isn't the reason we suffer emotionally because we are unconscious to the truth? Isn't that obvious?

Finally, we have the word FORGIVENESS. Actually all three known as CHOICE, RESPONSIBILITY AND IMAGINATION are leading to this most important of all known as forgiveness.

And the word forgiveness is also a reminder that since we have no choice and it is all imagination, then there's nothing to forgive. Therefore the word forgiveness is merely a reminder that there's nothing to forgive, and by doing nothing about that so-called emotional pain, we have entered Being and have expanded both our awareness and our love.

The highest practice in the spiritual arena is forgiveness. And yet, paradoxically, there's nothing to forgive. This means that as you start SEEING the truth everywhere, in every moment, you are expanding by leaps and bounds just doing nothing but SEEING.

The statement that I am BEING playing the human role is scary because it makes me feel that the human part is unreal and therefore I should avoid it and focus on the BEING. How do I use this understanding in daily life?

This statement covers the whole spectrum of the true Life. It doesn't demand anything of you which is not natural or normal. As you embrace this great truth into your life, it will become more comfortable when you start experiencing how easy life has become and so much freer and happier.

BEING is ultimate LOVE. Love has been called GOD, and religions have come out of this understanding when man was not yet awakened to its fullness. In brief, LOVE is not emotional or a need, but simply Oneness itself. It is all there is, and there is nothing else. Anything outside of love is misery, suffering, deprivation, loneliness, desperation, confusion and death.

When do you feel happiest? Isn't it when you feel fully alive? And what is that feeling, other than love? The world everyone experiences as real is merely a projection of the mind, and there's no love in it. This does not mean to escape from the world but to see it as it actually is – an expression of Spirit.

The truth which we want most, which is happiness, peace, love, joy, fulfillment, security and so on, cannot be had through the world of goals, plans, money and attainment, and that can be readily experienced.

However, again, this does not mean that we run away or deny them, not at all. The whole point is in seeing the truth as the truth. The forms are the projections of mind and are okay, but they cannot give us what we want. Our belief that the world can give us security and meaning is what causes our suffering.

I have realized that without peace of mind, nothing is worth it. Peace of mind is everything. Is there a way to acquire this peace?

You are right that peace is everything, however, there's no such thing as peace of mind. There is only the peace of God. The mind is thought (imagination). Since our whole world is the creation of thought (mind), peace is not part of it.

The peace of God is not only possible, but it is in this moment already, when we allow ourselves to see what is real and unreal.

The world cannot be real because it is all mind derived from imagination. Quantum physics has proved that matter is not real, but concentrated thought. The body itself, which we are attached to as who we are, is only real to our senses – senses derived from consciousness (mind).

There question could arise, "How do I know God exists?"

You don't. God does not exist. God IS existence Itself, known as nothingness or Spirit. Everything emerged from nothingness. If you see a gigantic oak tree large enough to make it into a home to live inside it, it is still an illusion brought on by nothingness.

That gigantic tree first was born from a seed. If you were to open that seed you'll find nothing there. That nothingness, which is the electromagnetic force of existence that sprouted that tree, is the very source from which everything emerged.

It is this nothingness (God), which is the Source. This Source is also Love, Peace, Joy and Fullness because they are the eternal nothingness Spirit. It is an Intelligence that boggles the mind. This is the REAL that created, out of itself, the extension of a Christ force, from which all human and animal life was possible.

The Peace of God is your birthright when you REALIZE that this world is not only an illusion, but ultimately it is not even "there." When you fully realize that this world is not real, with all its traditions, conditionings, religions, beliefs and mind creations, then you'll have a peace and freedom that truly surpasses understanding.

There can be no peace as long as you take daily existence (world) to be real and serious. The world is dualistic and this means that for every right there is a wrong, for every up there is a down, and for every here there is a there.

The internal and external of appearance is just appearance, and it is all imagination. When all this is seen clearly then that is the Peace of God that is also eternal. The Peace of God is our true Home and Heaven itself.

In your YouTube video #34 "What is negativity?" you replied to the question, "Does God exist?" You said, "God doesn't exist – God IS!" This has lingered in my mind, could you elaborate?

When we refer to something existing, it means it is visible, touchable, sensually perceived. Yet what is the source of existing things? Isn't it nothingness? Isn't it a pure essence from which everything emerges?

Before the universe appeared, there must have been a cause that brought it about, right? Was that cause a beginning? And if it was, then what caused it in the first place?

You see, we can go in circles trying to find out what the Source is. The fact is that Source is Causeless. This Causeless Source, which is beginningless and endless, cannot be defined simply because it caused everything, including Universal Mind. There is no way that the created mind can understand its creator. Therefore we can say that the Causeless Cause "just IS!" God IS!

CHAPTER TWENTY FIVE

THE GREATEST SECRET OF ALL

"IS"

The moment you FEEL the impact of this indefinable word IS, you have moved beyond words into the illimitable grasp of intelligence.

Right now, look at a blank part of the wall in front of you without moving your eyeballs. Just look at that blank space without blinking or moving the eyeballs and without thinking. What happens after five solid minutes of staring?

You'll feel a subtle feeling of stillness, silence, of pure Being. The staring into a blank wall might have seemed boring and senseless, yet after it was over you felt more relaxed and even happier somewhat.

Now imagine experiencing what the *Course* calls "The Holy Instant," where thought and the world disappeared temporarily. You would experience pure Awareness of the heart.

This cessation of thought and thinking opens the heart of stillness, which is the resident teacher of Truth. In Reality, there is nothing to know intellectually, but simply to enter emptiness or no-thingness.

In this seeming scary place for the mind is the secret of all knowing. In this nothingness there can be no fear, simply because there is no-thingness that triggers the emotion of fear. This stillness is beyond any stress, tension, fear, problem or any emotions known as unhappiness, worry, concern, self-consciousness or even doubt.

In this nothing state of BEING arises a feeling of okayness, also known as contentment. It is in entering this pure Being that we start **seeing** how happiness, peace, love, joy and fullness are our very true nature.

Our struggle in the world to achieve happiness and meaning always ends up bringing more misery than fulfillment. Yet the very thing we want most, believing it was in the world of form, was waiting for us in stillness of Being.

The word stillness is often construed by the mind as actionless activity. Stillness of Being can be experienced even in the midst of great activity once we start knowing this elusive word IS!

The ego part of us fears nothingness and even trembles at the very thought of it. Paradoxically, it is our true meaning and fulfillment as Being.

The sages, masters and mystics are the ones who have fallen in love with this spirit essence of nothingness. It is in this knowing that nothingness is discovered to be everything. It is truly the greatest secret of Life.

Does Oneness create every situation in my life? Has this Oneness created all the painful situations in my life to wake me up and see what is real?

Oneness does everything and IS everything. And although there is no such thing as my life, because there is no separation from Oneness, here's the paradox – you are Oneness!

Listen very carefully. Pause and hear this. There is no separation, period! It is like the One Vast Ocean and yet has billions of waves. Each wave is unique, different and seemingly separate, and YET it is all the same water.

We are this Oneness itself. We appear as a separate human being, but in truth we are BEING itself playing the human role. Therefore, what you do is the BEING (Oneness) doing.

In our evolution towards the realization of this Truth, we have seemingly separate interpretations of what seems to be happening.

It is this interpretation, based on our limited seeing, that creates the suffering.

When I was a teenager I felt alone and lonely. I would look at the bright stars and think, "How vast and glorious is space and yet I am so insignificant."

It was the interpretation of seeing my separation from this allness that made me feel lonely. Oneness marveled at itself through me, but it was my interpretation that turned it into suffering loneliness. Loneliness was a misguided seeing of vastness, believing it was out there instead of me.

How can I find lasting peace of mind in a world I don't understand?

There is no such thing as peace of mind. Peace is beyond mind and it is really the peace of God. The world you experience is one vast illusion. If you doubt this then let me ask you, "Can you think of anything that is real in this world?"

The values we cherish such as freedom, security, safety, love, happiness and fullness of being are IMPOSSIBLE in the world. Some people work hard all their lives and save money to be secure in their old age, and yet where's the security when the fear of disease, death and old age is ever present?

Therefore, there are two things that can ensure your peace. They are:

1. The realization that this world is a vast illusion. Nothing is real!
2. To forgive yourself the moment you make something real in this world.

These are the two necessary ingredients for lasting peace that truly surpass human understanding.

Listen to this statement – **Nothing is real!** What did you hear? Did you hear what is NOT real or what IS real? It all depends upon seeing the truth.

The Truth is that nothingness itself is real. Nothingness means that fear does not exist, because it is nothing. If fear is nothing then LOVE is real.

Oneness is love, joy, peace, fullness of Being. There is no beginning or end to Being. All is Spirit known as God. The moment we wake up to this fact, we will know a Heaven that truly boggles the mind of this world.

BURT HARDING

Burt Harding, founder of the Awareness Foundation in Vancouver, Canada, offers a radical invitation to recognize the truth of our being as already whole and fulfilled.

He reminds us of the love we really are beyond the personal stories we carry. In this way, we come to recognize what we have always known but did not live from – the beauty and wonder of our own true essence.

Burt conducts sessions and workshops in Supersentience, a system devised to help heal deep wounds and promote a shift in the perception of who we really are.

He has conducted studies in higher consciousness for thirty years and had his own television series on the mind/body connection.

Burt's web site is www.burtharding.com.